700WLW is proud to support
this special edition of
Willie – Radio's Great American:
The Story of Bill Cunningham
who can be heard weekdays from
Noon - 3 PM on 700WLW in Cincinnati,
and Sunday nights on
the Premiere Radio Networks.

WILLIE

Radio's
Great
American

The Story of
Bill Cunningham

BY **ERIC DETERS**
FOREWORD BY **SEAN HANNITY**

AP™
Acclaim Press
MORLEY, MISSOURI

Acclaim Press
— Your Next Great Book —
P.O. Box 238
Morley, MO 63767
(573) 472-9800
www.acclaimpress.com

Designer: Ron Eifert
Cover Design: M. Frene Melton

Library of Congress Cataloging-in-Publication Data

Deters, Eric.
  Willie-Radio's great American: the biography of Bill Cunningham /
by Eric Deters.
     p. cm.
  ISBN-13: 978-1-935001-31-7 (alk. paper)
  ISBN-10: 1-935001-31-0 (alk. paper)
  1. Cunningham, Bill, 1947- 2. Radio broadcasters--United States--
Biography. I. Title.
  PN1991.4.C865D48 2009
  791.4402'8092--dc22
  [B]

                              2009039842

Printed in the United States of America
First Printing: 2009
10 9 8 7 6 5 4 3 2 1

CONTENTS

DEDICATION

I dedicate this book to Willie's mother, Mary Ellen Cunningham. No one sitting in the pews of the church the day of her funeral and listening to Willie's eulogy could deny that Willie gives her all the love and credit a son can give. I have never heard a better eulogy.

Willie said, among other comments, that "Ma Cunningham" gave him the two indispensable values all good moms and dads give warmly to sons and daughters – roots and wings.

—Eric Deters

W ith all my love to Penny, Evan, Jennie, Cole and Avery ... without them, my life would not be worth living ... plus all my best to my buddies; I've earned a living by making money ... I've earned a life by making friends.

—Bill Cunningham

FOREWORD

I have known Bill Cunningham many years, having first met in Atlanta as we both worked in talk radio; he was already an established talk radio presence and my career was in the ascendancy. We have been buddies ever since and have only grown closer as the years roll by.

We share very similar views on the political, social and moral issues confronting America today. In fact, neither of us can recall a time or an issue where we fundamentally disagree. I asked him to be my guest on my previous Fox News Channel's *Hannity & Colmes* and now on *Hannity*. He got under the skin of Alan quite a few times, more than any other guest. I loved it. Now, I look forward to Bill crossing swords with Kristen Powers, Bob Beckel or Geraldo Rivera on *Hannity*. He is wonderful to watch.

What precipitated this book is John McCain's very public disavowing of Bill's comments at a campaign rally where Bill repeated a couple of times, now President Obama's full name — Barack Hussein Obama. This led to a break between the McCain camp and Bill, who is #1 on Cincinnati's 50,000-watt station, 700WLW. Bill was willing to move past it, McCain wasn't, and the result was failure in Ohio and losing of a national election.

Why do I know this? Because Bill, I and others traveled around the state of Ohio together for George W. Bush in 2004 and helped save the country from a John Kerry presidency.

Bill Cunningham would have and could have made a difference in Ohio in 2008. In radio and in this great country, he's already made a difference.

Yes, it's true, I did borrow from Bill, "You're a Great American." And, he does ask me about the royalties every time I see him.

Sean Hannity

INTRODUCTION

A few years ago I was having dinner with a contemporary of mine named Gabe Hobbs. Gabe is one of those visionary talk radio programmers who, as we like to say, *"Gets it."* After a few glasses of a really good and expensive cabernet sauvignon (someone else was paying for it), Gabe looked at me and said, "You know, one night we went to bed and woke up the next morning, and there was Rush Limbaugh. The next night we went to bed and woke up and there were 300 Rush Limbaughs (copycats of Rush Limbaugh). The third night we went to bed and woke up and there was conservative talk radio." We went on to laugh about how many people think talk radio has an agenda to push a conservative ideal. Gabe's point was that conservative talk radio just happened. It did. It wasn't planned. And I know you don't believe me.

Not too long after that I had the opportunity to talk at length with one of the people involved in the creation of *The Rush Limbaugh Show*, a fellow named Stu Crane. I asked him whether he had known Rush Limbaugh was going to be as big a hit as he was. He said he knew a lot of disenfranchised people in the country in the mid to late 1980s were tired of out-of-control government spending, a failing education system, and crime in the streets. He said he knew Limbaugh was resonating with people through his conservative message in, of all places, Sacramento, California, and if it worked there, it would probably work elsewhere and maybe on a nationwide basis. Of course, nothing was certain though.

It happened. The immensity *The Rush Limbaugh Show* became wasn't totally planned. And I know you don't believe me.

On a few occasions, I have been invited to be the guest speaker

9

and lecturer at a broadcast ethics class at the University of Cincinnati. Me, ethics! I'll usually grab something out of the media headlines and talk about that to the class – a class which is about to head out and become the next generation of journalists and radio and television personalities. The agenda of 700WLW, the station Bill Cunningham works for in Cincinnati, Ohio, always comes up. In fact, questions about "Willie" always come up too! As he likes to tell me and others, "I don't know if you realize this or not. But, half the people hate me."

I am normally asked questions that are phrased in ways that reveal the person's disdain for *The Big One* (700WLW's nickname) in that class or other public settings.

QUESTIONER: "I listened to 700WLW *by accident* a few days ago and I cannot believe you allow that Nazi, psychopath access to the public airwaves. Can you please tell me how you work to present a balanced viewpoint on *that* radio station, if you can call it that?"

DARRYL: "Psychopath? Nazi? I am not one for ad-homonym attacks."

QUESTIONER: "You know exactly who I'm talking about."

DARRYL: "Willie?"

QUESTIONER: "I won't lower myself to even say *his* name."

DARRYL: "What I'm about to say is going to upset you. But, here goes. There isn't a balanced viewpoint. We do not have daily meetings at noon to make sure we present a balanced viewpoint. We have one rule, and it's very easy to understand. Everything we do, everything we broadcast, every host understands it's about rule number one: *It's about ratings and revenue.* Get the largest number of people listening and sell commercials at the highest possible rate."

Students who are soon to be graduates primed to go out and change the world don't want to hear this. Nor do their professors. But, it's the truth. That's the agenda. And I know you don't want to believe me. You must. Rush? Ratings and revenue.

Keith Olbermann? Ratings and revenue. Willie? Yep. Ratings and revenue.

After Rush started to become a cultural *phenom* in the late '80s and early '90s, as Gabe Hobbs observed, there were hundreds of Rush Limbaughs. I'd get resumes and demo tapes (air checks in radio speak) and the cover letters invariably would say, *"I'm a conservative. But, I'm a different conservative from Rush Limbaugh."* If you need to say that, no you're not. Bill Cunningham would never say that. He doesn't need to. Like Rush, "Willie" *is* an original.

The truly gifted and talented in radio, television and broadcasting in general are originals. These are people who have taken their crafts of communicating to a whole different level. Being able to reach their level is something that is inside of a person and cannot be taught. A true entertainer, such as Willie, discovered his special gift probably by accident and exploits it to the joy of hundreds of thousands of listeners each day. Willie is no different from Rush. He is no different from the very talented and criticized (unfairly I might add) Howard Stern. I would also compare Willie to another original, Jerry Springer, whose talents are overshadowed by the guests and topics of his wild daytime TV talk show. "Jerry, Jerry" may be the best communicator in television today. He is commanding before a TV camera lens. Just as Willie commands an audience when sitting in front of a microphone, his unique voice broadcasts over 50,000 watts.

You see Willie cannot be called a radio talk show host. Willie is much more. He, like the others I mentioned, are entertainers. These are personalities who listen and whom viewers search out. Their fans want to know about their opinions, their lives, their likes and dislikes. The listeners want personalities such as Willie to entertain them and just spend a few minutes with them each day so they can smile and fall into simple escapism for a portion of their predicable day. They need Willie to make their mundane lives unpredictable.

I met Willie for the first time about fifteen years ago. He was doing the late night show on 700WLW, and I asked him if I could be in the studio with him one night to see how he crafted his radio broadcast. I was working at a sister station of *The Big One* at the time. The show started with his theme, George Thorogood's "*Bad To The Bone,*" a little after 9:00 p.m., and Willie started into the topic. There he sat in Studio A, slumped down in the oversized host's chair peering over his reading glasses. Across the table sat some boring bureaucrat who was there to discuss why people should approve some tax levy. The guest sounded like the teacher from *Peanuts* TV cartoon specials droning, "Wha, wha, wha!" Willie looked as if he could not have cared less about what the guy was saying. I sat to his side. After a few moments of this tax levy babble, Willie turned toward me with a sparkle in his eyes and yelled, "Wait a minute! Wait a minute!" At that moment the producer started the Elvis song *Viva Las Vegas*. Then the heavy, purple studio door flew open and in came an Elvis impersonator, singing. The guy didn't look like "The King," but he wore Elvis' trademark sunglasses and from the side rails of the shades hung sideburns. The bureaucrat sat stunned and speechless. Elvis finished the movie theme.

Willie turned back to the guy pushing the higher tax and said gently as if nothing happened, "Continue." The guest began his pitch again. As soon as he started, the next song began. That time it was Elvis' *Jailhouse Rock*. The faux Elvis began, "*Warden threw a party at the county jail! The prison band was there, they began to wail!*" Willie began to sing along, "*Everybody in the whole cell block was dancing to the Jailhouse Rock.*"

Once the performance had ended, it was time for a commercial break. Earlier, however, Willie asked the guest if there was anything else. He responded negatively and left. I wasn't sure whether he was bewildered or pissed. During the commercials, Willie, still slouched in his chair, turned his head toward me and said, "About every two weeks I like to do something really stupid."

I left that night realizing "Willie" was different. He was something special. He was an *entertainer*. He also taught me something that warm summer night, a priceless gift of knowledge for which

I can never thank him enough. That was the night I was able to truly say, *"I get it."*

Darryl Parks
Director of AM Operations
700WLW
Cincinnati, Ohio

PROLOGUE

*"We should not look back unless it is to derive useful
lessons from past errors, and for the purpose of
profiting by dearly bought experience."*

George Washington

As Bill "Willie" Cunningham strutted with the microphone
and fed the standing-room-only crowd at Cincinnati's
Memorial Hall all the political "red meat" he could throw,
the politicians on stage with him appeared pleased with his
performance.

Bill had been told by Republican officials to throw the faithful
some "red meat." On numerous other occasions beginning in the
1980's, red state conservatives called upon Willie to fire up the
crowds before the stage arrivals of Presidents and Republican candidates. For many months previous to this appearance on behalf
of John McCain, Willie opposed McCain's voting record, such as,
McCain — Feingold, McCain — Kennedy, McCain — Lieberman.
Since by February 25, 2008, it appeared likely McCain would be
the nominee of the so-called conservative party, Willie was asked
to fire up the selected, ticketed Republican crowd as he had done
for over twenty years.

Against his better judgment, Willie accepted and did his duty
on stage, as God gave him light to see that duty, to thunderous
applause. The gathered throng awaited the arrival of the Republican Presidential candidate, John McCain. As Willie left the stage,
his great friend Joe Deters yelled to Willie over the crowd "great

job." The crowd applauded with enthusiasm. Rob Portman, former Ohio Republican congressman and former cabinet member for George W. Bush, gave Willie the thumbs up.

Two young men with "McCain for President" stickers on their lapels told Willie he was "the best we've heard." Confident they were McCain staffers, Willie felt great about his performance. It was a job he filled countless times for the local GOP: Introduce a speaker and inject a little excitement in the campaign at hand.

Willie left Memorial Hall by the back door. He had paid a young man ten dollars to keep his SUV free of traffic. Willie jumped in his SUV and pulled onto Elm Street.

The time was a little before noon on February 25, 2008. Willie needed to reach Clear Channel's Cincinnati radio station headquarters to do his radio talk show on the "Nation Station," 50,000 watts — 700WLW AM, the midwest radio powerhouse.

As Willie drove up Elm Street, he looked in his rear view mirror. He could see the McCain auto entourage leading John McCain to Memorial Hall. A few protestors waved their signs across the street.

Believing all was right in his world, Willie was happy. Within thirty minutes, a national firestorm hit based upon the same remarks he made at Memorial Hall which were received so well by those in attendance. The televised remarks have now been viewed by tens of thousands on YouTube. In many ways the speech was prophetic about Barack Hussein Obama and the heated Presidential campaign ahead.

Whether he liked it or not, unexpectedly, Willie was going national.

CHAPTER I
WILLIE'S HERITAGE

"It's simply a matter of doing what you do best and not worrying about what the other fellow is going to do."

John Adams

On December 11, 1947, William Daniel Cunningham came into the world as the second child of William D. Cunningham and Mary Ellen Graham Cunningham. Both of Willie's parents grew up in the 1920s and 1930s in the small working class suburbs of Elsmere and Erlanger, Kentucky. As the "crow flies," these towns are ten miles south of Cincinnati, Ohio, across from the Ohio River in what is referred to as Northern Kentucky.

Mary Ellen Graham was one of four children. Her father, a postmaster, also served for a time as Mayor of Erlanger. "He dropped dead at age forty-two and left my grandmother and his four kids in the middle of the Great Depression without any means of support," Willie lamented.

Mary Ellen was only fourteen years old when her father died. Forced by the circumstances, she completed St. Henry's eighth grade and went straight to work. One of the highlights of Willie's mother's life occurred in 2002 when St. Henry's presented her an honorary high school diploma. The source of her pride was not simply the diploma, but that her four children were present as she received it, with tears in her eyes.

"She worked at various convenience stores. Her main job became Wright's Aeronautical which was forty miles north from home in Evendale. She helped build airplane engines there. Wright's is now General Electric," Willie explained with pride.

William Cunningham and Mary Ellen Graham met during World War II at a stateside dance when William came home on leave from Marine service. William actually fought in and survived the battle of Guadalcanal. Guadalcanal was part of the epic Pacific war campaign. The battle is often considered a turning point in the Pacific war. From the beach landing to victory, the fighting was fierce. William Cunningham was one of the fortunate survivors.

God would bless William and Mary Ellen with four children: John, now 64; Willie, 61; Patrick 58; and a daughter, Dianne Redden, now 55. All became successful under the watch, love and steady hand of Mary Ellen, their dear matriarch.

John is retired from the United States Government as an arbitrator with the National Labor Relations Board. Willie is a national radio talk show host. Patrick runs the Clairol division of the international consumer products giant, Procter and Gamble. Diane is a national sales manager for Lion's Apparel in Dayton, Ohio.

After World War II, William Cunningham worked at national grocer Kroger, and then consumer products giant Proctor & Gamble. Tragically, alcoholism consumed him. He couldn't keep jobs as a result of his love of the bottle. He was also convicted of numerous DUI's. In the 1950s, DUI awareness didn't even exist, and he was still repeatedly arrested, convicted and incarcerated several times.

"There would be stories in the newspaper about William Cunningham being picked up again. He was like the town drunk," Willie recalled with a small tinge of shame.

The Cunningham clan moved to Clifton, a Cincinnati suburb and then again to Deer Park, another suburb, when Willie was five or six. Deer Park would become home for Willie until he attended law school. It is also, to this day, where he received his identity as the "Voice of the Common Man."

CHAPTER 2

LITTLE PENNY ASBROCK

*"Patience and perseverance have a magical effect
before which difficulties disappear and obstacles
vanish."*

John Quincy Adams

In 1954, Willie attended the first grade at St. Saviour Grade
School in Deer Park.

"When I was a first grader, I had an accident in my pants early in the morning. I did a number two. I can specifically recall a nun walking around sniffing the room wondering what the hell was going on. I was in complete fright and utter terror. I was also embarrassed. In the first grade, with forty in the class, we had to ask the nuns for permission to go to the bathroom. I was scared to death of the nuns. I didn't know whether they were men or women or aliens. With their habits, they scared the hell out of me," Willie said with a laugh. The total control the nuns had over the St. Savior students was exhibited each All Souls Day.

Each year, the Catholic Church declares that countless souls dwell in Purgatory waiting permission to enter Heaven. Many, after death, found themselves not in Hell or Heaven but rather the rehabilitation center known as Purgatory. It's a place for those not living particularly holy or evil lives, but rather something in the middle.

Sister Monica Ann told Willie that it was his personal mission to free fifty souls from Purgatory by reciting six Our Fathers, six Hail

Mary's and six Glory Be's followed by a quick trip outside and then back into church. A short break had to preceed the process of healing another soul to give the incarcerated time to fly from Purgatory to Heaven. So each All Souls Day, religious St. Saviour students, on their free time, proceeded in and out of St. Saviour Church so that many souls locked in Purgatory could find peace with God. Sister Monica Ann promised Willie that he would later need the sacred intervention of these heavenly hosts when he died.

These "harmless" nuns were the Sisters of Charity who dressed in their full regalia every day. They wore black habits on their heads, and their gowns reached the ground. They dressed like "textbook" nuns. St. Vincent De Paul actually founded the Sisters of Charity.

In 1809, Elizabeth Seton, an American Saint, founded the first community of Sisters of Charity in Maryland. The Sisters came to Cincinnati in 1829 and became the first community of its kind in the Catholic Diocese of Cincinnati.

The Sisters served as nurses during the Civil War. The Sisters work has included education, health care and social services. Their vision statement included serving the poor.

In 1954, their vision was to mold Willie into a soldier of God and educate him in the Catholic faith. "I was scared to death because these nuns ruled by intimidation," he said. "Nobody talked. Nobody moved. It's a wonderful thing. I can specifically remember sitting there all day on a hot September afternoon afraid to move," Willie said.

"When I went home, I thought I'd be in trouble. Also, I didn't want anybody to know. If my brothers and sister found out, it would have been embarrassing. I told my mother and to my comfort she just said, 'Billy, I'll take care of you.' She took me into the bathroom, cleaned me up and never told anyone. She always protected me," Willie explained with gratitude and reverence. Mary Ellen would spend a lifetime looking after Willie.

Willie began a storied athletic career in grade school where he played all three of America's major sports: baseball, basketball and football. This led to his memorable meeting with his future wife, Penny. Penny would grow up to be the Honorable Penelope R. Cunningham of the Ohio Court of Appeals. However, before reaching judicial heights, Penelope was just little Penny Asbrock.

"I was the quarterback of the football team. Our big game at St. Saviour in the eighth grade was the Turkey Bowl against St. John's of Deer Park. Sister Monica Ann of St. Saviour pulled out of the ranks of the seventh grade, this little blonde-haired girl to lead the school in a cheer in a pep rally before the St. John's game. I thought she was a cheerleader, but she wasn't. That little girl was little Penny Asbrock. The cheer was like ocka locka aching, ocka lacka chung — St. Saviour. It went on and on."

"I sat with the team watching. I was an eighth grader. A little seventh grade girl did the splits in a little Catholic schoolgirl outfit. So I turned to Jack Monahan, my running mate to my left, and told him, 'I've got to put together a boy-girl party.'

"So we had our very first ever boy-girl party about two weeks later. My teammates asked me to call girls for them because they didn't have the cojones to call them themselves.

"Jack Monahan asked me to call Penny Asbrock for him. So I got the names of all the girls in the seventh and eighth grade and I called them all on behalf of my teammates to come to my house, in the basement, for a party.

"I put together some records and a record player. I boiled up some hot dogs. I sprung for some potato chips and pretzels.

"On Friday night at about six o'clock, little Penny Asbrock came walking down the steps to my basement wearing a diamond-like tiara and a chiffon dress. She was there for Jack, not me. When she walked down the steps, I was sitting at the phonograph with a hot dog in each hand. And unbeknownst to me at the time, before me was my future wife."

"Billy began to shepherd as many of the kids as he could to the laundry room because he wanted to play post office or spin the bottle," laughs Penny. Penny to this day calls her husband Billy.

"I told Sister Monica Ann I was going to the party. She actually warned me some of the boys would try to get me to play spin the bottle or post office and I shouldn't. So I didn't," Penny explained.

Willie, on the other hand, like most teenage boys, had no aversion to such games. But, as all teenage boys also know, they like the girls most who won't play the games — the girls you'd like to "bring home to Mom."

"Billy had them all organized. They were lined up," laughs Penny.

"I do remember Billy always had a big smile on his face, and he was always laughing about something or the other, I didn't know Billy existed, other than he called me to come to a party," Penny recollected.

According to Willie, Penny's mother and father thought she looked cute in a tiara and a chiffon dress. She was the only one dressed up at the party. Obviously, Penny's dress indicated a propensity toward a judicial robe. Everyone else at the party wore blue jeans.

"The dress looked like a First Communion dress. I played Elvis Presley songs and I remember playing "Wise Men Say Only Fools Rush In." I spent the night trying to slow dance with Penny," Willie admitted.

Penny kept rejecting Willie's advances, so he never had the pleasure that evening of holding Penny Asbrock in his arms. To Willie's chagrin, Penny danced the evening away with Jack Monahan. However, Willie would not give up pursuit for Penny Asbrock and would bide his time for another chance.

CHAPTER 3

A PUNCH IN THE GUT

*"I never knew a man who was good at making excuses
who was good at anything else."*

Benjamin Franklin

*I*n high school, Willie would continue his athletic exploits
in football, baseball and basketball. Moeller High School in
Cincinnati, where Willie would attend as a freshman, was actually
a new high school. Moeller is one of the many prominent Catholic
high schools in Cincinnati. The list of similar schools is long and also
includes Elder and Xavier. They each have strong academics and
have grown to be football powerhouses. Jerry Faust, former Notre
Dame University football coach, made Moeller a football institution
in the 1960s and 1970s. He had less success at Notre Dame.

When Willie enrolled in Moeller in 1962, the school was only in
its third year of existence. Willie kept up his grades and he quarterbacked the freshman football team. He also excelled in basketball and baseball.

Meanwhile, alcoholism overtook Willie's father the summer
prior to Willie's freshman year. According to Willie, he fell completely into the bottle. Willie's mother always remained at home
during the entire marriage to care for the four children even during the darkest times. The oldest child was sixteen that year. Willie was thirteen. The two youngest were nine and four. "She was
a typical World War II housewife. She didn't work outside the
home," Willie said of his mother's role.

Willie's father was getting drunk every day and became abusive to Mary Ellen. He was not as abusive to the children. "He was always my coach. When I played little league baseball, he was my coach and I had his name. So I was closer to him than the other kids were because I was the athlete of the family," Willie explains.

"We always did things together, but his alcoholism was just awful. He couldn't hold a job. Mom would get calls late at night to come pick him up out of bars. The neighborhood was embarrassed. A lot of arguing, fighting, screaming, and that kind of stuff went on. I used to lay in bed at night and listen to terrible arguments between Mom and Dad. I loved them both, especially my Dad, because I was really close to him," explains Willie of the typical confusion of the child of parents dealing with alcoholism.

"Mom told us the news one night at dinner. She prepared crepe suzettes which is fried bologna. She simply told us our Dad had left. I asked what she meant. She replied he was gone. I asked if he was dead. She replied, 'He just left.' I asked if he was coming back. She said she didn't know. From that point on, prior to my freshman year, I never saw him again the rest of my life. I never laid eyes on him," said Willie.

Years later, the Cunninghams discovered their husband and father had found his way to Illinois. He drove there and established another life. Fifteen to twenty years later, while Willie was married and living in Toledo, Ohio, Willie answered the phone at his home. The person on the other end of the line spoke:

"Bill, this is your father."

"How do I know you're my Dad?"

"Well, ask me a question."

"Who coached me at Rutger's Pharmacy?"

"Mr. Stein"

"Where are you?"

"Illinois."

"What do you want?"

"I'm dying of cancer. I've got cancer of the liver, and the doctor says I'm not going to live much longer. I have to see you. I want you to come see me."

"You weren't a father to me in my life, and I will not be a son to you in your death, so goodbye," Willie replied and hung up the phone. Willie called his mother and told her she wouldn't believe who called him. She already knew. Willie's father had called her to request Willie's number.

"What do you think I should do? What are you going to do?" asked Willie.

"I'm going to see him."

"Mom, you're going to see him after all he's done?"

"I have to go see him."

"Do you want me to go with you?"

"No you don't have to go. Diane and her husband will go."

"Look, if you want me to go, I'll go."

"You don't have to go."

"OK."

His father would call him once again to try to convince Willie to visit. Willie admits with regret he was cruel to his father during the conversation. But, who can blame a young man for having bitterness for his hero who abandoned him.

Willie's mother drove to Illinois to see her estranged husband. She reported back to Willie that his father was very disappointed because Willie hadn't joined her.

Willie calls his decision not to go one of the biggest mistakes of his life. He regrets he allowed his anger to get the best of him. On the radio, around Father's Day, Willie always tells the story of his father to assist others to make better decisions. So many times, serious breeches occur in parental/children relationships that appear insoluble, normally due to parental misconduct. Once death arrives, the breech is locked in place for eternity without resolution. Willie knows that not closing that wound when requested by his dad was a grievous error on his part that haunts him each Father's Day. What were the excuses/reasons for the desertion of his family? In the living years, Willie skipped the one meeting with his dad that would have resolved the issue. So, Willie always tells his listeners to accept or initiate meetings with estranged loved ones, especially mothers and fathers, before it is too late and causes unanswered questions to linger a lifetime. By the responses from the callers, many do.

Willie, in later discussions with his mother, would come to understand that his father's experiences hitting the beaches of Guadalcanal as a Marine led to the drinking. He came back from the war a changed man. That was a time when the mental health field didn't have the diagnosis "post traumatic stress disorder." They may not have had the label, but scars of war are scars of war in any era.

Willie recalls watching the movie *Saving Private Ryan* and realizing what his father and others must have experienced as they landed on beaches with fellow soldiers gunned down around them.

"Mom said before he went to the war, he was a great guy. When he came back from the war, he was different. I think it's impossible to kill, almost be killed and see your buddies blown up and not be affected. He was terribly affected. Some say alcoholism is a disease. I have my doubts. But nonetheless, I wish I had closed that chapter, and I wish I had gone to him and talked with him and let him verbalize about why he had been so abusive and left. I understand from Mom, he did remarry, but had no other kids. He worked menial jobs and died of alcoholism and liver cancer," said Willie. How can a father of four great kids with a beautiful wife miss graduations, weddings, births, Christmas mornings, July Fourth cookouts to say nothing of the beat of daily life — William Daniel Cunningham, Sr. gave it all away for what, a bottle of beer and a shot of booze.

Willie's father's alcoholism and abandonment of his family is a sad chapter in the family history, but it did not deter Willie from striving for his own future. There would be no excuses for Mary Ellen Cunningham and her four children.

CHAPTER 4

DEER PARK

*"The advancement and diffusion of knowledge is the
only guardian of true liberty."*

James Madison

*B*etween eighth and ninth grades, as the Cunningham's
household was in turmoil with the pains of alcoholism,
Mary Ellen faced the reality of having no money. "I don't mean a
little bit of money; I mean no money. Zero," Willie said.

Tuition to Moeller High School was a $100 a year. Mary Ellen
promised to pay $100 for Willie to attend one year at Moeller. Ev-
ery month, she would receive a letter from the school stating the
money was due. Next came repeated phone calls from the principal, Brother Larry Eveslage. Mary Ellen kept all this harangue
from Willie. It went on for nine months.

During the summer, before Willie's sophomore year, Brother
Eveslage informed Mary Ellen that Willie couldn't come back to
Moeller unless she paid the $100 back pay and the $100 in ad-
vance. In response, Mary Ellen, despite being a practicing Catholic
who had raised her children to be Catholic at Catholic schools,
told Brother Eveslage that Willie would not be back.

"So Mom told me about a week later that I wasn't going back
to Moeller. It was devastating. I had spent eight years in Catholic
School. I had friends from St. Saviour, St. John's and now Moeller.
I had done well academically and athletically, I said, 'Mom, why
can't I go to Moeller?'"

Willie considered Deer Park a step down on all fronts from Moeller. Mary Ellen told Willie she didn't care, he was going to Deer Park. Willie was embarrassed. The first day of school arrived and Willie asked his mother to go with him to Deer Park to register. Mary Ellen refused to go with him. Later, as a parent himself, Willie discovered that a "Mom" taking a fifteen-year-old boy to a high school would look bad; plus a mom knows that boys have to become self-sufficient, self-supporting men without protection from apron strings. Mary Ellen knew the "roots" were growing deeper and the "wings" were getting stronger.

"I was all alone and fourteen years old," Willie said. I walked to Deer Park High School, up the front steps, and up to the counter. My heart pounded; I was scared to death — I enrolled and began a new life," Willie recalls. All eight years at St. Saviour Grade School, Willie was educated by strict nuns without one lay teacher on the faculty. In his one year at Moeller High School, his instructors were from the religious order of Marianist Brothers, part of religious life. Deer Park was and is a middle class, practically all white high school in a middle class area of Cincinnati, Ohio, with decidedly non-religious teachers who were fine, but not nearly as strict or religious. The Great Awakening of the 1960s skipped Deer Park. Think of *Father Knows Best* and *My Three Sons*.

Willie began his Deer Park career in failure. He had a chip on his shoulder and apathy oppressed him. "I can recall there was something at Deer Park called Dummy Hall. If you flunked a class, you had to stay after school for a hour and study that class, I was a frequent visitor," Willie recalled.

Then came the day that changed Bill Cunningham's life.

John F. Kennedy was the youngest man and the first practicing Roman Catholic to be elected President of the United States. He had been the military commander of the Motor Torpedo Boat PT-109 stationed in the South Pacific during World War II. After the war, Kennedy pursued a career in politics at the urging of his father. From 1947 to 1953 he represented the Commonwealth of

Massachusetts in the U.S. House of Representatives and from 1953 to 1960 he served in the U.S. Senate.

In 1960, John Kennedy defeated the Republican candidate, Richard Nixon, in the presidential election. His short presidency was marked by adventure and crisis. The Cuban Missile Crisis, the building of the Berlin Wall, the Space Race, the African American Civil Rights Movement, and the beginnings of the Vietnam War kept President Kennedy occupied.

On November 22, 1963, Kennedy was killed by an assassin, and the nation was stunned. Lee Harvey Oswald was arrested and charged with the murder, but two days later he was killed by Jack Ruby before he could be tried. In 1979, the House Select Committee on Assassinations determined Oswald was more than likely involved in a conspiracy, but the topic remains controversial as theories about the assassination are still being debated. Kennedy is the only president to have been awarded the Pulitzer Prize with his book *Profiles in Courage* and remains possibly the most revered United States President.

"I was sitting in Dummy Hall after school because I had flunked Latin, especially painful for a Catholic boy," Willie said. "I hated Latin. I didn't want to be at Deer Park. I did not want to study and I did not want to take Latin. Then, at about 3:00 p.m. over the loudspeaker came the voice of Principal Louis Manning:

'I'm sad to inform you that President John F. Kennedy was killed this afternoon in Dallas.'

"It was November 22, 1963," Willie easily remembers the historical moment.

"As a Catholic boy in 1960, it was great pride to have a Catholic elected President. He received almost all the Catholic vote. Most Catholic homes had a photo of President Kennedy somewhere. We did. So there I was in Dummy Hall when Kennedy was assassinated. He would have hated where I was. So I said, that's it, I'm through with Dummy Hall. I'm going to succeed at what I'm going to do. So I cracked the books and graduated from Deer Park."

By his junior year, Willie realized the family had no money for college, and if he planned to go to college, he needed a scholarship. He also knew he would not be offered any academic scholarships. Willie spoke to Coach Jerry Wood, the basketball coach at Deer Park. It was hard to receive a baseball scholarship and Willie saw basketball as his opportunity.

At the time, Willie was five foot ten inches tall and weighed a hundred and fifty pounds. When he asked Coach Wood about a basketball scholarship, the coach told him he might have a chance if he worked on a few areas of his game: shooting, hustling and jumping.

"So over that summer," Willie said, "I took five hundred shots a day. I put weights on my ankles. I ran. I shot. All I did was practice. I quit the football team so I could focus on basketball."

"What are the odds of a kid 5'-10" leading the city in scoring, being first team All-City and getting a basketball scholarship?" Willie asked his coach.

"Not very good," Coach Wood responded.

Determined, Willie set out to do it. His senior year, he averaged twenty-five points a game, was first team All-city and received a basketball scholarship to Muskingham College in New Concord, Ohio, the home of astronaut and United States Senator John Glenn.

"That's how I got to college, because I had no other hope. What changed me was the assassination of John F. Kennedy and sitting in Dummy Hall," explains Willie.

In 2007, Willie was actually selected as one of the top 100 basketball players in the history of Greater Cincinnati/Northern Kentucky.

CHAPTER 5

LOVE AND MARRIAGE

*"There is a certain enthusiasm in liberty that makes
human nature rise above itself in acts of bravery and
heroism."*

Alexander Hamilton

Willie attended Muskingham College for a year and a half on a basketball scholarship. He played varsity basketball as a freshman, but in the middle of his sophomore year, love diverted his attention from Muskingham. In December of his freshman year, while home on Christmas break, Willie attended midnight Mass with his mother at St. Saviour Church in Deer Park, Ohio. Five pews in front of Willie, off an aisle seat, stood Penny Asbrock. Willie had not laid eyes on Penny since grade school. Penny actually recalls Willie always having a heightened interest in her cousin, Barbie Asbrock, not her.

On December 24, 1966, Willie was nineteen and Penny eighteen. "I looked up and said, 'Damn, she's cute!' And when she turned around, I saw it was little Penny Asbrock. She had grown up a little bit over the last four years."

Penny also recalls the Midnight Mass.

"Actually I was with a couple of our friends. I was a senior in high school, and a couple of our friends had come to our home and we all decided to go to Midnight Mass. So I was there. My mom and dad were going to go to Mass the next day. So my sister and I and two of our friends went to Midnight Mass. And by the time we got there, we were a little late and there were no pews available, so we stood along the wall in the aisle. And as I recall it, Billy said he saw me from the back. My hair was long. He waited until I went up to communion and when I turned he saw who I was and recognized me from grade school. I hadn't seen Billy through high school. I went to one basketball game when he played at Deer Park High School. My cousins and I went in there one night to watch a basketball game and I saw him on the court. I saw his mother, who, as I understand it, went to every one of his games. When I saw her in the stands and recognized her and I knew that was Billy, but other than that, I had not seen Bill for four and a half years," Penny recalls.

The next night Willie realized that he needed a date for the reunion of his high school baseball team. At home after Mass at 1:30 a.m., he searched in the phone book for Penny's number, questioning himself whether or not he should call her at 1:30 in the morning.

As he is prone to do, Willie threw caution to the wind and called her. "Her father answered the phone and wanted to know why I was calling his daughter at one-thirty in the morning," Willie said. "He was kind of angry." I explained I had just seen her at church and thought she'd still be up. He thought it was nice that I had seen her at church since that meant I too had been to church. So he called her to the phone. We talked, and I asked her out. She accepted. We went on a date the night after Christmas. Things progressed quickly over the next eight to nine months so I didn't want to go back to Muskingham away from Penny," Willie recalls.

Penny has a funny take on the date.

"I got on the phone and said hello," said Penny.

"Cunningham here, is this Penny?"

"Puzzled, I wondered who the heck he was? Then I remembered. He asked me out the next day to a baseball reunion. I didn't have anything planned, so I said sure," Penny recalls.

Penny had dated someone who was in the Navy; but she wasn't engaged or going steady, so Willie's timing was perfect.

31

"The night that he came to pick me up on the first date, I had not seen Billy since he was in the eighth grade," said Penny. "Now he was a freshman in college and I thought, well, sure, we'll go out and see what's changed. But when I opened up the door, he was standing there wearing the *same hat* he had in grade school, the same *coat* he had in grade school. And I thought *what have I done, it's eighth grade all over again. What am I doing?* He had an Irish walking hat on. He loved that hat, and when Billie loves something, it stays with him forever. The coat that he was wearing was *plaid*," Penny laughed at the memory.

"What had happened was, he loved that coat so much that his mother bought him the exact same coat for Christmas the freshman year in college. I thought, *oh, my God, he hasn't changed at all. He hasn't changed at all.* But we had fun. He made me laugh. He still makes me laugh," said Penny.

"By December of the next year, Penny and I were getting hot and heavy," Willie said. "She told me we weren't having sex until we got married, so I decided we had to get married."

Willie spoke to his mother and decided he had to transfer back home.

"Mom, I don't want to go back to Muskingham."

"Well, you're crazy."

"Yeah, but I want to marry Penny."

"Wait until after college."

"I can't wait. We have to get married."

In January 1968, Willie transferred to Xavier University in Cincinnati. He registered at the registrar's office and was accepted. However, he had no money.

"I went and saw the baseball coach and basketball coach because I had used two years of eligibility in Muskingham. I only had one year left. The basketball coach told me he didn't need me. I went to the baseball coach, Joe Hawk, and thanks to a recommendation from Hal Pennington, with whom I played summer baseball, Hawk gave me a partial baseball scholarship," explains Willie.

Willie's ingenuity continued. He visited a manager of the

apartment building and convinced him he could be a resident manager. That resulted in $40 a month rent rather than $80. Next, Willie went to work at U.S. Shoe Company filling orders in Norwood in Cincinnati, Ohio.

"In September of 1968, Penny went to Florida with some girlfriends. I picked her up at the airport. She was gorgeous with a beautiful tan. I immediately drove to Getz Jewelers to pick up an engagement ring, which I laid away with no money. I asked the clerk if I could use it for one day and bring it back because I wanted her to wear it when she showed her mom and dad. The clerk trusted me to take it away and bring it back. That evening, we went to Penny's parents. Penny, her five siblings and mom and dad lived in a three-room house," recalls Willie.

Both of Penny's parents had eighth grade educations. Her mother stayed at home. Her father worked at Formica. Penny was the oldest of six. She attended St. Peter and Paul in Reading her first five years in school. After the sixth grade, the Asbrocks moved to Rossmoyne where Penny attended St. Saviour for the seventh and eighth grades. She and Willie share the common bond of uneducated parents in terms of formal education, paycheck-to-paycheck fathers and stay-at-home mothers. None of that precluded them from being great parents.

"My father worked extremely hard and my mother worked very hard inside the home. We grew up on three rooms until I was almost fourteen," Penny recalls.

Penny attended Mt. Notre Dame High School.

"Billy picked me up at the airport and drove to Getz Jewelers which, at that time, was in a little shopping center. I wondered, why we were going here. Billy took me back and showed me a ring that he'd been looking at. I was very surprised," Penny said.

"I wasn't expecting that. I was only nineteen and I knew my father would be very upset. I had always told my parents that I wasn't looking to get married until I was in my twenties. I wanted to travel and do some things. So that evening, when Billy did get the ring, we went to my family's home," said Penny.

When Willie and Penny walked in the house, the Asbrock

family were sitting around the kitchen table. Penny tucked her ring finger behind her leg; then, she pulled her arm up to show the family her ring and said, "Take a look at this!" Willie stood next to Penny beaming with pride and happiness. Penny's father, a former U.S. Marine, looked at Penny (his pride and joy), looked at the ring, looked at Willie and said, "You've got to be kidding me. This is a joke."

"So we were just left standing there. The sisters looked at the ring as if to say — 'you're marrying this guy?' They couldn't believe it. They thought Penny had lost her mind. I left a little dejected and Penny stayed home," recalls Willie.

"He never said another word to us the rest of the evening. That was it. I knew he was upset. And then the next morning at breakfast he apologized," Penny said.

A couple of days later Rick Asbrock sat down with Willie, apologized, and asked how Willie planned to support his daughter. "I didn't have much to lay out," laughs Willie.

"It was that I was so young, and Billy was a little out of the norm from the guys I dated, so they didn't know quite how to take him," Penny explained.

The Cunninghams were married at St. James in Wyoming in Cincinnati on January 25, 1969. Willie was twenty-one and Penny twenty. Jerry Green, the co-captain with Willie on the baseball team at Xavier, was his best man.

The couple got off to a rough start beginning with the wedding itself. As the blushing bride, in a borrowed gown, was slowly walking up the aisle on her father's arm in a packed Catholic church, Willie's face turned white as chalk. The music was playing, the pressure was building and the solemnity of the proceeding was bearing down on him. An exit door was about ten feet behind Willie as he and his best man waited at the altar. Willie's eyes stared at that door, then back to Jerry Green who quickly said, "Don't you dare — we're staying right here." Willie truly considered bolting.

Penny recalls the priest mispronounced her name during the ceremony. As the new couple walked out of the church, Willie stepped on the train of her dress and tore it. When the confetti and rice was thrown as they left the church, the confetti struck in her eyes. As Penny cried, mascara streamed down her cheeks.

"That all happened and we hadn't yet made it to the reception!" Penny recalled.

Based upon the financial circumstances, the reception was humbly at the VFW Hall in Blue Ash, a suburb of Cincinnati. They planned no honeymoon because they had no money. They spent the night at the Holiday Inn in downtown Cincinnati. More problems followed the couple there.

"When we arrived, we got out of the car and Billy asked me to hold his suit coat. We walked into the lobby and went up to our room. Maybe a half hour or so later, Billy realized his wallet was gone. It had every dime we had in the world, including close to $500 people had given us at the reception. Billy had taken the money at the end of the evening and put it in his wallet. Now the wallet was gone! I guess when I had taken his suit coat and put it over my arm, the wallet had slipped out. We were beside ourselves, but we called down to the front desk and, fortunately a gentleman had turned in the wallet, and every single bill was in it," she said. "There must be a God."

Penny worked as a secretary at General Electric in Evendale before marriage. At that point, she had not attended college. Her supportive father drove her to work every day.

When Willie graduated from Xavier in 1970 he decided he would become a golf pro. He caddied a lot of golf and played pretty well. He played at Sharon Woods and actually won the club championship a few times.

"I thought I was pretty good at golf. So I said to Penny, 'Look, if I don't pursue this dream, later in life I'm going to be real unhappy for not having tried.'"

"What do you want to do?" she asked.

"I want to drive to Florida," he replied.

"Where?"

"I don't know. Let's go to Miami."

"I liked Miami because I had liked Miami University in Oxford,"

Willie said. "So we put everything we owned in our VW bug, got in the car, and drove from Cincinnati to Miami, Florida, in about a day and a half. We pulled into Miami, said 'okay, we're here'; but nobody cared. In a week, we found a place to live. I found a job at Kings Bay Yacht and Country Club. Penny took a job with the dean at the University of Miami in the law school. I spent about two months hitting and picking up golf balls. I was like a range boy. I was able to play golf and hit balls; but I discovered from that experience that I wasn't very good at all. These other kids could hit the ball out of sight and putt like crazy. My golf dream was over!"

The dean of the law school at Miami suggested Willie attend law school. Willie had always thought about law school because of his love for *Owen Marshall* and *Perry Mason*.

Owen Marshall was a legal drama on ABC from 1971 to 1974. Arthur Hill played Owen Marshall, a defense attorney practicing in Santa Barbara, California. Two of his television assistants were David Soul, later of *Starsky and Hutch*, and Lee Majors, later of *Six Million-Dollar Man*.

Perry Mason was the fictional attorney on television based upon Erle Gardner's stories. Perry Mason's clients, charged with murder, would always stand trial. Inevitably, Mason would prove his client's innocence by proving another person's guilt. This usually happened at the end of the trial during cross-examination. In one story, Mason responded to an accusation he only stuck up for criminals with this response: "I never stuck up for any criminal. I have merely asked for the orderly administration of an impartial justice. Due legal process is my own safeguard against being convicted unjustly. To my mind, that's government. That's law and order."

The *Perry Mason* television series appeared on CBS and ran from 1957 to 1966. Raymond Burr played Perry Mason. Della Street was the name of Perry Mason's secretary and Paul Drake was his private investigator. Watching this team always win made an impression on Willie.

The dean helped Willie receive acceptance into Stetson College of Law in St. Petersburg Beach, Florida. Willie began law school in

1971. After the first year, the young couple returned to Cincinnati for the summer.

"I said to Penny, look, if I don't apply to an Ohio or Kentucky law school, we're never going to come back home. I applied to all of them and only Toledo admitted me. So I went to Toledo Law School. We drove to Toledo in our VW bug," explains Willie. He would graduate from law school in 1974.

Penny supported the young couple while Willie pursued the legal profession. She worked as a secretary at General Electric, University of Toledo, University of Miami Law School, Hartford Insurance and U.S. Shoe Corporation.

"I can type pretty fast," laughs Penny.

At Toledo, Penny became a steward for the Ohio Civil Service Employees Association where she presented individual grievances against the University and represented their cases.

"After that, I became President of the Employees Association while I was still working as a secretary there and as an administrative assistant," Penny said.

Penny delayed college, but she would graduate from the University of Cincinnati, where she received her undergraduate degree in 1984, Summa Cum Laude, and her law degree in 1987. She was appointed to the Hamilton County Domestic Relations Court in 1995. Penny won election to the position in 1996 and was re-elected in 2002. In 2006, she was elected to the First District Court of Appeals. She has served on the Ohio Supreme Court. Before being elected to the bench, Penny also kept a private practice and served as an Assistant Hamilton County Prosecutor. She is a past officer and Trustee with the Ohio Association of Domestic Relations Judges. She has been a member on the Domestic Relations Law and Procedures Committee for the Ohio Judicial Conference and has served on several committees and educational panels for the Ohio Judicial College. Penny also held the office of Chair for the Mount Notre Dame High School Board of Trustees after serving as a member of the Board for more than five years. Penny was a member of the first class admitted into the Notre Dame Hall of Fame for her numerous accomplishments.

Willie believes his wife has a "legitimate" life while he doesn't. Unlike conservative talk radio, Penny listens to National Public Radio. Once, before she sentenced a man to jail, he asked her if she would get him Willie's autograph. The entire courtroom laughed. Penny looked down at him with little humor from behind the bench and said: "I'll tell you what. You need my signature more than you need his." She then threw him in jail with her "autograph" on the order.

CHAPTER 6

EVAN — THE ONLY BEGOTTEN SON

"I love the man that can smile in trouble, that can gather strength from distress, and grow brave by reflection."

Thomas Paine

*P*enny and Willie have one child, their son Evan, born October 29, 1972. The physical act of childbirth is always easier on men: God made it that way. This fact proved itself with Evan's birth. After thirty hours of hard labor, baby Evan arrived. No female name had been selected because Penny was certain she would have a boy. Willie and Penny agreed that Penny would have naming rights. Before sonograms, the gender of the baby at the moment of birth was one of life's great discoveries. In those days, fathers were not permitted, at least in Toledo Hospital, Ohio, to enter the delivery room itself. No argument arose from Willie. He spent every minute at his wife's side until "the moment" arrived. Penny was wheeled into the delivery room and a couple of hours later she exited, exhausted and exhilarated, with baby at her side.

"How are you felling now?" Willie asked.

"Not good," replied Penny.

With that, she opened a white towel and said, "It's Evan."

Willie unwrapped baby Evan to count all the body parts and

found that all was well. For all parents, the birth of their first baby is a life-altering moment of incredible joy. Before leaving the hospital, Willie went to the nursery area to check on Evan who was sleeping with other newborn infants in a small room under the watchful eye of a nurse. By then it was 2:00 a.m.

Willie told the nurse that his son was "right there" so could he hold him? The nurse said that it was against the rules, but that she would turn her back. Willie picked up his son, placing one hand on Evan's forehead and said, "For all the days of my life, I will give you unconditional love. Through all the good times and bad, through the years, no matter what, I will be with you until the day I die. I will be to you the good father I never had." As Willie left the hospital, tears streamed down his face.

The next four years in Toledo, Ohio, were, in retrospect, difficult. Willie worked in Lucas County Common Pleas Court as a Constable to Judge Robert V. Franklin from 8:00 a.m.to 4:30 p.m. daily and then attended the University of Toledo Law School from 6:00 p.m. to 10:00 p.m. four nights a week. This schedule went on for four years. Penny worked 8:00 a.m. to 5:00 p.m. at the University of Toledo as a secretary and union organizer. Time spent with Evan was precious, but each had places to go in their careers with a defined path.

"After Evan was born, Billy never thought of watching Evan as babysitting. He was right there feeding, changing diapers and bathing," explains Penny. "When we lived in Toledo," Penny continued, "we were preparing to come to Cincinnati for the Thanksgiving holiday. I was packing while Billy washed Evan in the baby tub. Suddenly I heard coughing and flailing going on, and I ran into the kitchen. Billy had washed Evan's hair but didn't realize that babies didn't know how to hold their breath. He was dunking him in the water to rinse off his head," recalls Penny.

"What's wrong?" Willie asked.

"Oh my God. Billy, babies don't know how to hold their breath. You can't dunk him."

"He was drowning me," Evan says now. "He almost killed me."

Willie often coached his son in sports. Sometimes he was the head coach, and other times he would be an assistant. Evan played football, baseball, basketball and soccer as a student in Moeller and Madeira High Schools. When Evan was thirteen or fourteen, one of his team sponsors was Bob Crable, a big burly man, six feet tall and three hundred pounds. Crable was a linebacker who played for Moeller, Notre Dame and the NFL. Evan's team was sponsored by his company Crable Sportswear. Crable didn't coach the team; another big guy did. Somehow, Willie learned that coach had a history of pedophilia.

"He got this guy and practically tore his head off, Evan said. "He was gone the next day and we had a new coach."

That event wasn't the only time Willie defended his son. Once after a high school game, a man confronted Evan. The man was in an uproar.

"I left the arena before I was supposed to, and the man turned out to be the father of a teammate on this team," recalls Evan.

The man grabbed Evan by the neck.

"It is not your turn to go!" the man yelled.

"Get off of me," Evan responded.

Then all hell broke lose. Everyone tackled the man. The police came. Evan went home with a red neck. He was pretty shaken up.

When Willie found out what happened, he set out to find the perpetrator.

"Dad had no idea who he was. It was an away team that came to the city, but Dad found the guy in a day or two," laughs Evan.

After Willie found him, he sued him and obtained a few bucks for damages.

"Dad would travel from one end of the spectrum to the other. Overall, it was a really good time growing up. He was funny. We went to movies and ate a lot of pizza. But when he got mad, look out," Evan says now.

Evan acknowledges that he was spoiled. Yet, he maintains that life was not always a bed of roses because his parents pursued their careers. "I did always have snacks," laughs Evan.

Willie hates vacations. The radio station where he works,

700WLW, has created "fights" between Willie and his sidekick Segman Dennison so he could be "suspended." He's famous for always returning early from vacations. His 2008 vacation to his "double-wide," as he calls his condo in Naples, Florida, involved Hurricane Faye striking and delaying his return by two days. For those two days, Willie called the radio station periodically live on the air to provide weather updates including standing in the storm doing his best Geraldo Rivera imitation.

Evan recalls Myrtle Beach as a favorite destination when he was a youngster. Willie could golf and Evan enjoyed the waves. The long car trips involved a few light-hearted moments. Evan recalls one when he was twelve.

"Dad hated to pull over when I had to use the restroom. He refused to pull over. I was in the back seat behind him and some friends were with us. To spite me, he made me pee in a cup. It was a McDonald's cup. I was embarrassed because I was with my buddies. He made me pee squatting and putting the cup between my knees. I filled the cup and then asked him what I should do with it. He told me to throw it out the window. I rolled down the window and threw it, but the wind blew it back in. It went all over Dad's head and eyes. He was dripping in my pee. My buddies and I were rolling!" laughs Evan.

Evan is married to Jennie. They have a five-year-old daughter, Avery, and a son, Cole, who is six. When Cole was six weeks old, Willie and Penny began a Friday night ritual of babysitting their grandchildren overnight. They do so today without exception. Avery and Cole are the lights in Willie's life. Like most new grandparents, Willie and Penny had no idea that being a grandparent would be so enjoyable. One never envisions oneself as a "grandparent." It sounds so old. So, to avoid the label, Willie and Penny decided to be called Poppie and Nana. The experiences of being in the hospital during their birth and the closeness of Evan and Jennie to Willie and Penny caused close and deep love for their two grandchildren. In their presence, Willie becomes a drooling, babbling idiot servant carefully watching every move. Willie loves being a grandfather — pure and simple.

"We are very fortunate to have parents who love being with our children," Evan says with gratitude. To quote Evan, it makes it easy that Evan and Jennie live a "three iron" from his parents.

In 1999, Evan began work at Clear Channel radio in sales. Clear Channel owns 700WLW where Willie works. At the time, the station was on several floors in Mt. Adams in Cincinnati. Later, it was moved to one floor in Kenwood, a northern suburb of Cincinnati. "It was nice working at the same place as Dad," Evan added. "It was a good time. We got to be together and work together. It was the first time we had that kind of experience." Evan would later leave Clear Channel to run Willie's reemergence in the restaurant business.

CHAPTER 7
ALWAYS IN TROUBLE

"The Constitution is colorblind, and neither knows nor tolerates classes among citizens."

John Marshall

Willie's athletic leadership landed him the co-captaincy of the Xavier baseball team. The coach, Joe Hawk, scheduled a ten-day tour of the south during spring break. The team would play in Mississippi, Alabama, and New Orleans. During a game, as Willie was playing second base, an opposing player hit a groundball to third in a double-play situation. As Willie pivoted for the relay to first, the runner coming into second barreled into him. He struck Willie's leg and Willie went flying into the air. Willie thought he had broken his leg. They drove him to the local ER where they x-rayed his leg. Fortunately, he suffered a deep bruise instead of a break.

Four days later, Willie announced to Coach Hawk that he was ready to play again. With a big bandage on his left lower leg, Willie returned to his second base position. With a runner on first, a batter for Delta State hit a ground ball to shortstop. The shortstop flipped the ball to Willie. Before Willie could turn and throw, the base runner wheelbarrowed into him knocking him down as he flipped over. Willie held onto the ball as he fell to the ground. He tells the rest of the story:

"I got up with the ball still clutched in my hand. He was still on the ground. I looked down at him and he started to smile. So I threw the ball as hard as I could at him. It nailed him on the nose from a distance of about three feet. Blood flew everywhere out of his nose. Then, the entire Delta State team charged me at second base. I looked to the right for my guys, thinking I'd stand my ground. My guys didn't move. They had abandoned their captain. I turned and ran toward centerfield. I reached the outfield fence, which was ten feet high, and started to climb. As I reached the top, they arrived at the fence. I dropped to the other side and ran into the woods. With my uniform and glove, I hid in the woods for a couple of innings. Then I sneaked around back to the dugout. I yelled at my guys for not coming to my aid, but Jerry Green, the co-captain, and the guys said they were laughing so hard, they couldn't move."

The picture of Willie running for his life with an entire baseball team chasing him is too much. Anyone who knows Willie's style on the radio would appreciate the picture. In Willie's senior year at Xavier, a double-header was scheduled in South Bend, Indiana, against Notre Dame. That year Xavier was terrible. They had won only five games and the Fighting Irish were pretty good. That game would be their last road trip of a long season. The night before the game, Coach Hawk called Willie to inform him game time had changed. He had to call the other players so they would be at Schmidt Fieldhouse by 6:00 a.m. Saturday for the van trip to Notre Dame. Dutifully, all the calls were made, but the players expressed displeasure at the thought of arising at 5:00 a.m. to leave at 6:00 on a four and a half hour van ride to South Bend to play baseball in six hours. Then they had to travel four and a half hours back. Displeasure was expressed in the form of "Hell no" and "Well, I'm not going" and "You're nuts."

The next morning only seven players reported for duty. Coach Hawks was livid and berated Willie for his failure to gather the Xavier team for the big double dip at Notre Dame. On the way out of town, one of the two cramped vans stopped at players' apartments until two more were gathered for the trip. Xavier played with nine men. Incredibly, they won one of the games on a double by Willie to left center, which knocked in two runs. After the

45

second game, the Notre Dame coach had his team running out-field grasses, from left field foul line to right field foul line, as pun-ishment for losing to such a terrible baseball team. The trip back to Cincinnati was much shorter than the early morning trip had been, and the lights in the Golden Dome were dimmed.

For fun on a Saturday night radio show I was hosting on 700WLW (November 2008), I held a contest for the James Bond of Greater Cincinnati. The new Bond movie *Quantum of Solace* had recently opened. Willie was doing well in the race for the esteemed prize as radio callers called in to vote. When Willie called in, we decided he had to be removed from consideration because he's never been in a fight. You can't be James Bond if you don't fight.

From childhood to teenage years to and during his adulthood, Willie had never been in a physical fight. "My fist has never land-ed on someone's face. I've always been able to talk my way out of the noose," laughs Willie.

He's been in situations where he thought he'd be hit, but al-ways avoided the confrontation. He has received threats and had to call security a few times.

He acknowledges there are those who hate him and sometimes verbally attack him. He simply acknowledges their opinion and says, "The hell with them."

"I can get more angry with Willie than any other person I know. He's lucky there are no knives at my finger tips sometimes," Pen-ny laughs.

An example of Willie's provocation is his propensity to make de-cisions without speaking to Penny first. This has manifested itself a few times with Willie selling their homes without her input!

"He sold our previous home and I didn't know it until I got the phone call telling me. He has a tendency to do such things. He may come home with a new car that he just purchased and I've never seen before," said Penny.

Just a few months ago, Penny received another surprise.

"I was talking to him on the telephone and I heard someone say to him that they had the tape measure. He asked me what kind of floors we have in the kitchen," said Penny.

"Well, they're bamboo. Why? What's going on? Somebody has a tape measure? Why do they have a tape measure?"

"Well, so and so from so and so is here measuring all the rooms."

"Billy are you saying our house is going to be listed for sale? Did you list our house for sale?"

"Well, it's going to be by owner, but yes, I did and I've got the sign."

"I'm going to pull in from work tonight and see a sign to sell our house!"

"Well, I decided that this morning."

Willie had his better moments too. Penny continues, "On our 35th wedding anniversary, or a few months after, Willie gave me a great surprise. On Easter weekend, I had my parents, Evan and the kids, and other family members over to the house. Everyone except my parents had left. I was going to drive them home and we were getting ready to leave."

Willie walked into the room and said, "Why don't you wait for a moment. Why not take a seat in the family room. I have something here and I want you to stay for a moment."

He left the room for a few minutes. When he came back, Willie walked over to Penny and kneeled down on one knee in front of her.

He opened up a ring case and said, "We've been together thirty-five years. I want you to know how much I love you and I'd like you to renew my contract for another thirty-five years!" Penny relates that story with pride.

In 2008, Penny received the opportunity to sit on the Ohio Supreme Court. She received a call from Chief Justice Moyer's office asking if she would be available to sit as a visiting judge. One of the justices had to recuse him or herself from the case. As it turned out, she wasn't on the panel for her Court on that day, so she was wide open and pleased to receive the invitation. The case involved insurance and a civil matter, not criminal. A proud and supportive Willie did not do his show so he could travel to Columbus, Ohio, and watch his wife serve on the state's highest court.

"He's my biggest fan," Penny says.

In the summer of 1967, after Willie completed his freshman year of college, he and a buddy named Bob Arnzen decided to hitchhike to Las Vegas. After several days and an equal number of rides later, they arrived worn out in St. Louis, Missouri, under the Gateway Arch. Deciding to abandon their quest by hitchhiking, they called Bob Arnzen's mother, who purchased airline tickets for them. After flying to "Sin City" and hanging out for a while, they moved on to Los Angeles, California. There they saw a band everyone knows as "The Doors." Willie recalls leaving the bar because The Doors kept playing the same song, *Light My Fire*, over and over. Willie left Arnzen behind in LA and decided to hitchhike back to Las Vegas.

As he stood outside a LA hotel, a limousine pulled up. A guy got out and struck up a conversation with Willie. It was Joe Esposito, one of Elvis' Memphis Mafia. Esposito asked Willie where he was heading. When Willie told him he was traveling to McGarran Field in Las Vegas, Esposito offered him a ride. Willie readily accepted. When Willie jumped into the limousine and sat down, in front of him sat the King, Elvis Presley! Wiillie had the opportunity to shoot the breeze with Elvis as he rode with the Memphis Mafia to Las Vegas.

After arriving in Vegas, they dropped Willie off at the airport and Willie said goodbye to the King. To this day, Willie is an Elvis fan. He hired an Elvis impersonator to entertain at the opening of his Independence, Kentucky, Willie's Sports Café in 2007. He also always honors Elvis' birthday and death anniversary with songs on his show.

CHAPTER 8
1968

*"To stand in silence when they should be protesting
makes cowards out of men."*

Abraham Lincoln

*T*om Brokaw recently wrote a book and produced a
documentary called *1968*. It is a brilliant account of what
may be the most turbulent year in U.S. history.

If you look at 1968 – day by day, the events which took place,
both culturally and politically seem beyond remarkable. They included all of the following:

1. Viet Cong and North Vietnamese launched the Tet Offensive in Vietnam.
2. Thirty-two African nations boycotted the Olympics.
3. Robert McNamara resigned as Secretary Of Defense.
4. President Johnson announced he would not seek
   reelection.
5. Howard University students seized an administration
   building.
6. We went off gold standard.
7. General Westmoreland was fired.
8. Students seized a building at Bowie State.
9. Martin Luther King was assassinated.
10. Riots broke out in 76 cities.
11. The Civil Rights Act of 1968 was signed.

12. 178,000 employees of the U.S. Bell Telephone System went on strike.
13. Students seized buildings on Columbia University campus.
14. Students seized an administration building at Ohio State University.
15. Ten million workers went on strike in France.
16. FBI- escalated attacks on "dissenters" occurred.
17. There was a "Poor Peoples March" on Washington – 50,000 marchers.
18. Andy Warhol survived a shooting.
19. Robert Kennedy was assassinated.
20. Chief Justice Earl Warren resigned.
21. Race riot in Gary, Indiana.
22. Race riots in Miami, Chicago and Little Rock.
23. 650,000 Soviet Union and Warsaw Pact troops invaded Czechoslovakia.
24. France exploded a hydrogen bomb.
25. Violent protests at the Democratic National Convention in Chicago.
26. Major earthquake in Iran - 12,000 died and 60,000 buildings were destroyed.
27. Army Coup – Congo
28. Hijackers killed 21 people on a Pan Am jet.
29. Bloody massacre in Mexico before Olympics.
30. Riots – Catholics/Police – Northern Ireland.
31. The Olympic Committee suspended Tommie Smith and John Carlos for giving "black power" salute at medal ceremony.
32. London riots against Vietnam War.
33. "National Turn in Your Draft Card Day" featured draft card burning.
34. Zodiac killer struck.
35. Israel attacked an airport in Beirut.
36. U.S. Stock Market began decline of 44% over 18 months.
37. Detroit newspaper strike closed both daily papers for 267 days.

Is it ironic that 1968 was also the year O.J. won the Heisman?

In 1968, Willie was on the verge of college graduation and beginning married life.

"At Xavier, I thought America was going to go through a second American Revolution," Willie said. "It was ugly. Kent State. The Tet Offensive. A thousand boys a week were killed in Vietnam."

The Vietnam War ran from 1956 to 1975. The war was fought between the communist Democratic Republic of Vietnam (North Vietnam) and its communist allies and the U.S.-supported Republic of Vietnam (South Vietnam). It concluded with the defeat and dissolution of South Vietnam; and North Vietnam violated the 1973 cease-fire agreement and invaded the South in 1975 after U.S. forces withdrew

Over 50,000 U.S. soldiers lost their lives in Vietnam. Hundreds of thousands more of them had their lives changed forever as they returned with injuries, disabilities, post traumatic stress and an unsympathetic public.

The war was already an issue before 1968. Then the North launched the Tet Offensive.

The Tet Offensive is named for the date it began, January 31, the lunar new year holiday in Vietnam. The military campaign was conducted by the Viet Cong and the People's Army of Vietnam. The purpose was to strike the civilian and military command throughout South Vietnam. It was the largest offensive by either side up to that point. The offensive was not a military success, but affected the war in American public opinion. It shocked Americans who had been led to believe the Viet Cong were being defeated.

Kent State became the poster for political and civil unrest of the 1960's. On a Monday morning on May 4, 1970, the Ohio National Guard shot students in Kent, Ohio, on the Kent State University campus. Four students died and nine were wounded. The violence occurred while several students protested the American invasion of Cambodia.

The national response included hundreds of universities,

colleges and high schools closing due to a student strike of eight million students.

Martin Luther King, Jr. was a Baptist minister who came to be one of the most influential leaders of the Civil Rights Movement in America. He began as a civil rights activist early in his career and served as the first president of the Southern Christian Leadership Conference, which he founded in 1957. His efforts in the movement lead to the famous March on Washington in 1963. It was tere that he gave his "I Have a Dream" speech which raised public awareness of the Civil Rights Movement. It would go on to become one of the most well known speeches in American history. After the Gettysburg Address, I consider it the best speech ever given on American soil. It also established King as one of the greatest orators in the history of the country. In 1964, King became the youngest recipient of the Nobel Peace Prize for his efforts to end segregation without violence. On April 4, 1968, King was assassinated in Memphis, Tennessee. In 1977, President Jimmy Carter awarded him the Presidential Medal of Freedom and in 1986 Martin Luther King Jr., Day was established as a national holiday.

Robert (Bobby) Kennedy was one of President John F. Kennedy's younger brothers and served as the U.S. Attorney General from 1961 to 1964. He was one of President Kennedy's most trusted advisors, and worked with him closely during the Cuban Missile Crisis. Bobby Kennedy also made considerable contributions to the African American Civil Rights Movement. Bobby Kennedy continued as the U.S. Attorney General for nine months under President Johnson, following the assassination of his brother. Disagreeing on the Vietnam War and other issues, Bobby resigned in September 1964. By November of the same year, he was elected into the U.S. Senate from New York. In early 1964, Bobby announced that he would contend for the Democratic Party nomination for President. On June 4, 1968, he defeated Eugene McCarthy in the California primary. Just after midnight, on June 5, 1968, Sirhan Sirhan assassinated him as he walked though a hotel kitchen. He died the next day on June 6. President Johnson declared June 9 an official day of mourning.

Vietnam, Kent State, Martin Luther King, Jr. and Bobby Kennedy assassinations, and all the rest, caused many to believe that America was coming apart.

Willie recalls sitting outside the resident apartment building at Xavier with a shotgun in his hands. A friend joined him. The black community was burning down large parts of Avondale in Cincinnati. The owner of the building, Eric Bose, was concerned because his building was in Avondale. Bose told Willie to get a gun and go sit outside on the front lawn on a chair and see if he could keep the building from being burned down.

"So I and a buddy sat there with shotguns in the front of that little apartment building because it was student housing. It was a private building, but all the residents were students," recalls Willie.

Willie recalls a large number of African Americans walking and running up the street, but they left the building alone.

"A large number of army reserve trucks with machine guns were going down Dana Avenue during the riots because Xavier was in the middle of the black community," Willie recalls.

"We watched television like everyone else. Major cities were burning. Vietnam. RFK assassinated. Martin Luther King assassinated. At Xavier, Jesuits marched around campus with dismissal slips. The word went out that if anyone did anything wrong at Xavier, that student would be expelled. The University of Cincinnati shut down."

Willie and America would survive 1968. Willie would graduate from Xavier with a Bachelor of Arts in history and then face the draft.

CHAPTER 9

PRIVATE CUNNINGHAM

"In every battle there comes a time when both sides consider themselves beaten, then he who continues the attack wins."

Ulysses S. Grant

The American colonies had variations of a draft during the American Revolution. President James Madison tried a draft during the War of 1812. The north instituted a draft during the Civil War. It touched off the New York Draft Riots in July 1863. The Confederacy tried a draft, and it too faced resistance.

It was President Franklin Roosevelt who signed the Selective Training and Service Act of 1940 and created the country's first peacetime draft. From 1948 to 1973, men were drafted to fill vacancies in the armed forces.

A lottery drawing was held on December 1, 1969, at Selective Service National Headquarters in Washington, D.C. That event determined the order of call for induction during calendar year 1970 for registrants born between January 1, 1944, and December 31, 1950.

Three hundred and sixty-six blue plastic capsules containing birth dates were placed in a large glass jar and drawn by hand to assign order-of-call numbers to all men within the 18-26 age range specified in Selective Service law.

With national radio and television covering the event, the capsules were drawn from the jar, opened, and the dates posted in order. The first capsule, drawn by Congressman Alexander Pirnie (R-NY) of the House Armed Services Committee, contained the date September 14. This meant that all men born on September 14 in any year between 1944 and 1950 were assigned lottery number 1. The drawing continued until all days of the year, including February 29 for leap year, had been matched to lottery numbers.

In 1973, the draft ended and the U.S. converted to an all-volunteer military, which remains today.

A man could qualify for a student deferment if he could show he was a full-time student making satisfactory progress toward a degree. A conscientious objector was an individual whose personal beliefs were incompatible with military service. Some also refused military service for religious reasons. This did not apply to Willie. In the United States, during the Vietnam War, many used political connections to be placed away from the "hot" war. Willie didn't have any of those. Many avoided military service through college deferments, by becoming fathers, or serving in various exempt jobs. A medical rejection was also a way out of a ticket to Vietnam.

People who were drafted and who attempted to simply not go were known as "draft-dodgers." During the Vietnam War, U.S. draft-dodgers usually made their way to Canada or Mexico. Many people looked upon draft-dodgers with scorn and thought of them as cowards. Others supported their efforts. Today, American men between the ages of 18 and 25 are required to register with the government, but there has not been a call-up since the Vietnam Era.

In 1969, Willie recalls watching Lieutenant General Hershey on television when the draft was initiated.

At the time, Willie was in the Xavier Army ROTC as Lieutenant Bill Cunningham. Willie and many of his Xavier friends gathered in Willie's apartment on the appointed night. "The general put all 366 possible days in a metal round bin and began rolling that thing and pulling out the dates that would induct men into the armed services," Willie says. The scary apprehension gave way to gallous humor as number after number was yanked from the lottery-like basket. As a student's birthday was called, others hummed taps since 1,000 American boys were killed in that worthless war. Willie's birth date, December 11, 1947 received a low number.

Willie recalls that since his birth date was in the 40s, it meant he would be drafted. The news reported if you were below 150, you would probably be drafted. "So all the young men between the ages of 18 and 26 were in front of the television set that night, because it meant they might live or die. So I had a little party in my apartment with the other residents," Willie recalls.

It was live on television. All three networks, ABC, NBC and CBS, carried it. The military needed more bodies in Vietnam and Willie was a senior in college.

"About two weeks later I received an induction notice from the United States Army which stated: 'Greetings. We are pleased to inform you that you have been inducted into the Armed Services of the United States of America.'" Willie laughs at the "pleased to inform" phrase. He was told to report on a particular date to the Federal Building in downtown Cincinnati.

"The form stated that if anyone had a reason he should not be inducted, that person should bring that information with him," Willie said.

Willie had a back condition for which Dr. Elmer Schlueter gave him a letter. On the date given, Willie rode the bus to downtown Cincinnati. There he, along with many others, went through eight hours of testing in white sweat socks and underwear. Willie recalls a cold linoleum floor. They sent Willie through eye, ear, flexibility, mental and character tests. At the end of the tests, Willie lined up with twenty other "lucky" young men. A rock-ribbed Army sergeant yelled out, "Any of you SOB's have one of those bullshit letters step forward." A line of about fifteen future soldiers ready for the Vietnam meat-grinder stood at attention. Willie knew that the "letter" was in his pants hanging on a hook several feet away. After a pregnant pause, slowly yet with determination, Willie took one decisive step forward, standing at attention. The sergeant walked over to Willie, nose to nose, and said, "You son of a bitch, get out of my sight, go there and go there now," pointing to a hallway with one small office at the end.

A captain sat there writing. Willie related the event. "He cussed at me and told me to sit down. I sat on a cold Samsonite® chair. He asked for the letter and I gave it to him. For thirty minutes, he continued writing and flipping papers. I sat at attention. At the end of thirty minutes, he handed me back my letter, cursed at me and told me goodbye. I retrieved my stuff and went home." Dr. Schlueter had diagnosed Willie with spindylothesis, a misalignment of the spine resulting in a lack of flexibility and causing pain.

Willie then met with Colonel Dooley and Major Tessler, his commanding officers in the ROTC, and showed him the letter. "They told me there was no reason for me to be in ROTC if I couldn't serve. I quit ROTC!" recalls Willie.

Some of Willie's friends were killed in Vietnam and he thinks about what his fate may have been but for his "bullshit letter." There have been rumors by "Willie haters" that he went to Canada. To some he was Sasbatcheram Willie. Not true. He received a medical rejection.

CHAPTER 10

RUNNING FOR POLITICAL OFFICE

"There are no easy answers but there are simple answers. We must have the courage to do what we know is morally right."

Ronald Reagan

When Willie registered to vote at age eighteen, he registered to vote as most Catholics in the 1960s registered, as a Democrat. Willie became a Kennedy Democrat. He would later run for public office twice as a Democrat.

"Because of John F. Kennedy, I kind of always thought I would get into politics. I was so impressed with him," explains Willie. As political junkies know, Bill Clinton claims shaking hands as a young man with JFK changed his life. As we have learned, JFK changed Willie's life while Willie sat in Dummy Hall listening to the news of the President's assassination over the public address system at Deer Park High School.

After law school, Willie moved back from Toledo, Ohio to Cincinnati. He looked up John Socko Wiethe, the Hamilton County Democrat Party Chairman, and told Wiethe he'd like to become active in politics. "He liked me and took a shine to me," Willie remembers.

Wiethe is a legend. In the 1930s, he coached the Cincinnati Bengals. It is from this early pro team Paul Brown took the name the

Bengals when he won a NFL franchise in the late 1960s. Wiethe also played professional football in "leatherhead" style. Wiethe placed Willie in a job with the Ohio Attorney General's office. Then, Wiethe asked Willie to run against a woman named Helen Fix, a Republican in the 26th House District in Hamilton County. Willie readily accepted. The year was 1978. Willie was appointed as an Ohio Assistant Attorney General under William J. Brown. He represented the Workers Compensation Fund when injured workers tried, in Willie's view, to drain workers compensation benefits to which they were not entitled. Some may say that Willie kept workers from getting their rightful benefits, but Willie would defend himself by claiming that by precluding fraudulent or boastful claims, adequate compensation would be always available when a rightful injured worker had a compensable claim.

"Being a Democrat and running for office in the Cincinnati suburbs of Indian Hill, Madeira and Loveland was probably not my smartest move. It was ten to one Republican, even then. But I came up with a motto that I thought would carry me to the top," Willie said.

Willie's motto was "The Fix is in. Get the Fix out. Vote the man. Vote Cunningham." Willie's campaign, $1,200 in funds, and his motto gained a disappointing twenty-eight percent of the vote. The "Fix" received seventy two percent and remained in office. It was not the political debut Willie had envisioned.

The following year, 1979, a group of political insurgents wanted to take over Madeira City Council, a small suburb of Cincinnati. Willie joined the insurgency. Five ran. Four were to be elected. Willie believes he finished sixth. Willie has not sought political office since. He has pondered a congressional race in the past. However, he has chosen to remain behind the microphone rather than in front of a political podium.

"You know, it was fun," Penny said. "I think the people we had around us were a lot of fun. We had a lot of energy and Billy was on a mission!"

Like Willie, Penny, once a Democrat, is now a Republican.

Chapter 11

Switching Parties

*"America was not built on fear. America was
built on courage, on imagination, and unbeatable
determination to do the job at hand."*

Harry Truman

Willie has always been conservative. He's pro-life, pro-family, pro-defense and pro-military. By the late 1970s Jimmy Carter, George McGovern and Ted Kennedy were the dominant national figures in the Democratic Party.

Jimmy Carter served two terms in the Georgia State Senate before becoming Governor of Georgia. He served as President of the United States from 1977 to 1981. Although a nice man and smart captain of a nuclear submarine, Carter was a weak President. While in office, he created two new cabinet departments: the Department of Energy and the Department of Education. Carter was unable to make the U.S. less dependent on foreign oil, but managed to establish a national energy policy and remove price controls from domestic petroleum production. He came under scrutiny for agreeing to give up the Panama Canal. In 1979, he negotiated a peace treaty between Israel and Egypt and aimed to make human rights more of a priority. However, by 1980 his approval ratings had dropped significantly. The American embassy in Iran was taken over by Iranian students who took hostages. There was a botched attempt to rescue them. The nation experienced serious fuel shortages, the Soviets invaded Afghanistan and interest rates and unemployment rates were double digits. Carter's failed presidency helped persuade Willie to become a Republican.

Carter lost the 1980 presidential election to Willie's hero, Ronald Reagan. Since leaving the Presidency, Carter has traveled the world promoting global health and human rights. He is a leading figure for Habitat for Humanity and in 2002 was awarded the Nobel Peace Prize. He was still a lousy president.

As Ronald Reagan stated, "I didn't leave the Democrats. The Democrats left me." Willie feels the same way.

"After Ronald Reagan won the presidency in 1980, I found myself closer to him than Ted Kennedy. The reason I switched parties was a personal belief that the Democrats were on the wrong track. That continues through today. I'm a member of the Reagan Revolution," explains Willie.

A Kennedy brought Willie to the Democratic Party and a Kennedy helped send him over to the Republican side.

Ronald Reagan served as President of the United States from 1981-1989. Reagan was an actor, president of the Screen Actors Guild and a spokesman for General Electric. Originally a member of the Democratic Party, he switched his party allegiance to the Republican Party in 1962. It was his speech in support of Barry Goldwater's 1964 Presidential campaign which launched Reagan's political career. He was elected Governor of California in 1966 and again in 1970. He lost the Republican presidential nomination in 1968 and 1976, but won in 1980.

As President, Reagan chose to lead with a policy of limited government and economic laissez-faire. His supply side economics included substantial tax cuts in 1981 which pulled us out of recession. In his first term, he survived an assassination attempt. He also ordered a military action in Grenada and Libya. He won 49 states in 1984 in a landslide victory reelection over Walter Mondale.

During his second term, Reagan publicly portrayed the USSR as an "evil empire" and supported anti-communist movements worldwide. He ordered a massive military buildup and held an arms race with the Soviet Union. He told Mikhail Gorbachev to tear down the Berlin Wall as Reagan stood in front of it. His famous meeting in Geneva with Mikhail Gorbachev is considered the moment when the Cold War would end and the Soviet Union would begin its transformation. Reagan left office in 1989 and later that year, under his former Vice-President, then-President George Bush, Sr., the Berlin Wall fell and so did the communist Soviet Union.

Diagnosed in 1994 with Alzheimer's, Reagan died in 2004 at age ninety-three.

"I loved Reagan because no matter what the circumstances, he made me feel better to be an American. Whether it was the *Challenger* explosion, Grenada, Libya, Gorbachev, or whatever he handled, I was proud that he represented America so well. He held a vision with a core set of beliefs not governed by the popular whim. He wrote brilliant speeches. He could express the English language like no other. He was magnetic and charismatic. I fear the Republicans will search in vain for the next Ronald Reagan. It's like trying to find the next Abraham Lincoln," Willie believes.

The first American space shuttle was the *Columbia*. The *Challenger* was the second. NASA first launched the *Challenger* on April 4, 1983. It flew nine missions. It broke apart seventy three seconds after the launch of its tenth mission on January 28, 1986. All seven crew members died: Ellison S. Onizuke, Sharon Christa McAuliffe, Greg Jarvis, Judy Resnik, Michael J. Smith, Dick Scobee and Ron McNair.

I summarize Ronald Reagan's presidency by believing it was like it would have been if John Wayne was President. Ronald Reagan and John Wayne were both actors and are both icons in America. One political icon and one on the silver screen, but both are still representative of what America stands for: strength and righteousness.

Willie maintains he is a conservative, not a Republican. He is probably closer to a libertarian conservative. That's the label I give him. He can be very critical of Republicans.

In 2006, Willie told Kathy Wilson of *Cincinnati* magazine, "Some of the worst Republicans are Jack Abramoff and Tom DeLay who fly around on private jets and play golf in Scotland and tell me about family values." Willie was critical of Ohio Governor Bob Taft who ran the state in the ground. Taft pled guilty to a misdemeanor while still in office. Willie also soured on President Bush's handling of Iraq and allowing the "fat cats" on Wall Street to place America in economic peril. Willie is no party line man.

In 1983, the switch from Democrat to Republican mirrored Willie's arrival in talk radio. Since the national and local media lean left, a radio talk show is the bellwether that counterbalances CBS, NBC, ABC and major network newspapers. Talk radio gives listeners exposure to conservative philosophies not otherwise heard, seen or read. Since most Americans are moderate to conservative, many gravitate to talk radio to confirm their general conservative views or to fill in the blanks not covered by mainstream media.

CHAPTER 12

WILLIE'S SPORTS CAFÉ

*"Twenty years from now you will be more
disappointed by the things that you didn't do than by
the ones you did. So throw off the bowlines. Sail away
from the safe harbor. Catch the trade winds in your
sails. Explore. Dream. Discover."*

Mark Twain

*A*fter Willie's father left town, Mary Ellen, his mother, went to work. She worked at the Marriott Hot Shoppes in the Kenwood Mall. When she applied for a job, Willie went with her. The building lacked a ceiling and the entire shopping mall was still under construction. Marriott hired Mary Ellen as a line cook in a cafeteria style restaurant in which she would serve food as customers walked down the line. Mary Ellen was the first employee hired.

Mary Ellen would remain employed in the same restaurant for twenty years. She became line supervisor because she could work longer hours and they didn't have to pay her as much. She worked six days a week for ten to twelve hours a day. Never weighing a hundred pounds her entire life, she handled large pans of hot food with ease. Willie also applied at the Marriott and became a bus boy.

"She stood on her feet the entire time behind the line, serving people. She did it with dignity and respect. She did not miss one day of work in twenty years," Willie states with pride.

(Above) William Daniel Cunningham and Mary Ellen Graham as they marry, July 5, 1943.

(Left) Willie (on left) and his brothers, John and Pat, as well as Mary Diane, his sister.

(Above) Mary Ellen's three boys.

(Right) Willie's fourth grade picture.

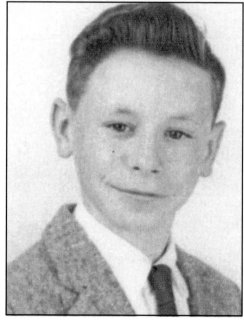

Willie and a fellow "angel" at First Communion.

Willie and a buddy dress for some football.

Penny Asbrock at Mt. Notre Dame High School, Reading, Ohio.

Tammy Asbrock, Penny's sister.

(Above) Willie in high school (still has the plaid jacket!).

(Left) A newspsper article dated February 24, 1966, details Willie's performance as the leading scorer among Cincinnati high schools during his senior season at Deer Park.

Willie and Penny at his Xavier University graduation.

Penny in a cave at the age of 20.

Willie playing catch.

Willie in his R.O.T.C. uniform (1969).

Willie and Evan.

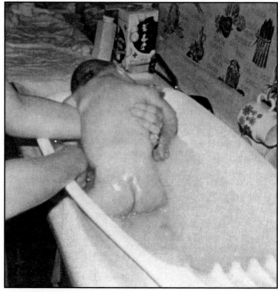

Evan gets a bath.

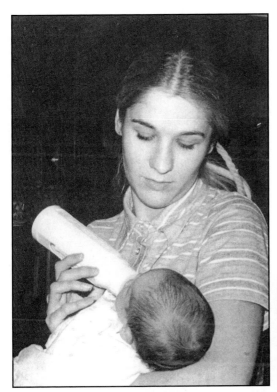

(Above left) Penny with Evan.

(Above) A pregnant Penny.

(Left) Willie and Evan.

(Above) Willie with relatives of Penny.
(Below) Willie with his son, Evan.

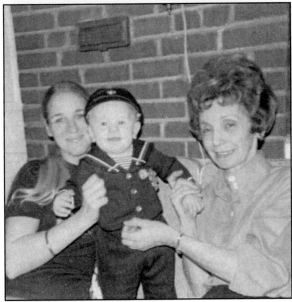

(Above) Cunningham family portrait, 1978.

(Left)   Penny, Evan, and Mary Cunningham.

Sean Hannity (far right), Ken Blackwell and Willie.

Willie, Penny, Cole and Avery (2005).

(Above) Evan and Jennie Cunningham at their wedding (2000).
(Below) Willie and Evan as they win the Father/Son Golf Tourney at Kenwood Country Club.

Willie, Penny and her secretary.

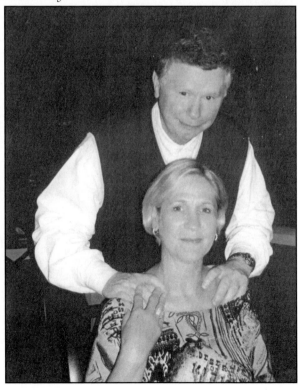

*Willie and
Penny.*

(Above) Willie and his grandson, Cole.
(Below) Willie, Penny, Jennie, and Evan at Judge Penelope R.Cunningham's Judicial Investiture.

Willie and his mom in 2006; she died February 5, 2008.

A corporate decision by Marriott Hot Shoppes to shut down their cafeteria-style concept, resulted in Mary Ellen losing her job. Mary Ellen had become the dominant character and dominant personality of the restaurant.

"When she left and they shut down, the manager, Tom Kessinger, gave my mom the honor of hitting the light switch for the last time as they shut the door," said Willie.

Willie spent many days as a bus boy at the Marriott before it closed. He would visit his Mom there, too, after he stopped busing tables in college and law school. "The restaurant business was in me," explains Willie.

In 1987, Willie thought he would transfer his "alleged" popularity or notoriety from the radio to the restaurant business. "I thought I knew it. I found out I didn't," he admits with a laugh.

With several of his buddies and an architect, Dennis Cronin, Willie led an expedition to Columbus, Chicago, and Detroit to scout sports bar concepts. He returned to Cincinnati with a stack of photos, menus and ideas. While sitting in the grill of the Kenwood Country Club, Willie spoke to Bobby Walsh, who planned to build a strip mall in Kenwood. Willie spoke to Walsh about opening up his first Willie's in the mall.

Willie convinced a few friends to put up $500,000 dollars. Bill Brisben, Barry Bucher, Marty Wolf and Mike McCall, along with Willie, opened the first Willie's in 1988. Willie added locations in Covington, Kentucky, Western Hills, Ohio, and West Chester, Ohio. Four Willie's opened between 1988 and 1996. Willie's is a typical sports bar, but includes photos of Willie with famous people everywhere. Patrons can drink, eat and watch the big game.

"I was practicing law, was on the radio every night from nine to midnight, and running four restaurants like a CEO with two hundred employees. I was busy," Willie said.

The restaurants were successful. They had combined sales of six million annually. In 1998, one of the managers, Brad Orr, approached Willie about purchasing the West Chester location. Willie told Brad if he were to sell, it would be all of them. Brad came back to Willie a year later claiming he had the money and financial backers. Willie sold. He and his investors netted a few bucks. Brad would later add two more locations of Willie's. Willie still receives a little money for the use of his name.

The first customer in Willie's first store was Willie's mother. "My Mom served the first beer at my first Willie's," Willie remembers.

"The restaurant business is tough, but we weren't afraid to take the risk. We put the time in, but always felt we had our law degrees to fall back on. We are entrepreneurial. We told ourselves that if it didn't work and we lost our shirts, tomorrow's another day. We'd start over again," Penny explains. "Anyone who has been in the restaurant business knows it's a risky endeavor. My father, a banker, once told me that the definition of a successful restaurant is one that pays its bills."

Willie laughs about the insanity of going back into the business.

"I must be nuts," he says.

CHAPTER 13

WILLIE THE LAWYER

"The supreme quality for leadership in unquestionably integrity. Without it, no real success is possible, no matter whether it is on a section gang, a football field, in an army, or in an office."

Dwight Eisenhower

*I*t was unbelievable that, after law school, Willie was able to first practice law at the law firm in Toledo of Schnorf & Schnorf Co., LPA. The firm has been in business since 1936 and was led by Brandon Schnorf and his son, David. The firm focused on insurance, banking, and labor law. Willie developed an active practice doing mainly corporate legal matters and a few criminal cases.

"So every day (all day long) I would hear, 'Good morning, Schnorf, Schnorf & Schorf' from the receptionist as she answered the phone," Willie remembers.

While in law school, Willie worked as a bailiff during the day and attended law school at night. He worked as a bailiff for four years in the Lucas County Common Pleas Court, swearing in witnesses and reading jury verdicts. He went to law school at night from six to ten p.m. After four years and graduation, Willie passed the Ohio Bar exam on his first attempt. The judge Willie worked for in Lucas County was Judge Robert V. Franklin, who had been a roommate of Martin Luther King, Jr., at Morehouse College. *Black Enterprise* listed the college as the number one college in the nation for educating blacks. The college was established in 1867 as the

Augusta Institute in Atlanta, Georgia. The primary purpose was to prepare graduates for teaching or ministry. More black men have received bachelor degrees from Morehouse than any other college or university in the country. More than 40 states and 12 foreign countries are represented in their current enrollment over over 2,000 students. Judge Franklin entertained and inspired Willie with stories about Martin Luther King, Jr.

For years, Judge Franklin was the only black judge elected in Lucas County. Before Willie knew he had passed the bar, the judge appointed him to a criminal case, confident that Willie would pass. Willie came through and passed to prove Judge Franklin's confidence was not misplaced. The first case Judge Franklin assigned to Willie was the defense of a man accused of assault with a deadly weapon.

"I had watched the Owen Marshall and Perry Mason stuff. I'd watched trials first hand for four years, hundreds of trials. So I thought I could try a case," Willie explains.

"I learned that doing it and seeing it are completely different. But, I came up with a trick in my first case. The assault with a deadly weapon was allegedly a butter knife. I had twelve jurors in the box. I was very young. And when I gave my closing argument after about a day and a half trial, all the bailiffs and clerks that I had worked with were in the back of the courtroom. Even some of the judges from Lucas County, Judge Kiroff and Judge Glasser came to watch. I was the constable at the courthouse. I was a personality and they liked me. They wanted to see how I did in my first closing argument. I thought I was an expert because I had seen it all the time."

"I held that butter knife over my head, in my right hand, as I strutted in front of the jury, wearing the only suit I owned. I took that "dull" butter knife and slashed it across my left palm in order to prove it was not a deadly weapon and that it could not cause harm to anyone. Well, a butter knife can cut flesh. I laid my hand completely open. I felt the blood flow from my left palm. Blood was going everywhere. I put my hand into my pocket to try to hide it from the jury."

"About three minutes later, Judge Franklin asked me to approach the bench," states Willie.

"Ladies and gentlemen of the jury, we need a few minutes here. Would you go in the jury room," Judge Franklin instructed.

"So he got the twelve jurors out, and I walked up to the bench. Franklin started to laugh, and the court reporter was there.

Judge Franklin asked, "You laid it wide open, didn't you?"

"Yes, Judge, I did."

"Let's go into my chambers."

"So we went into chambers, I opened the palm of my hand, and there was a cut about three inches long and a quarter inch deep. It was bleeding badly," recalls Willie.

"He said, 'Let's go,' put me in his car, and we drove to the Toledo Hospital emergency room. I received eighteen stitches in the palm of my left hand and a bandage. The prosecutor died laughing, running all over the Lucas County Courthouse," Willie recalls.

"The bailiff, the constables and the whole courthouse was laughing at me. And I was thinking, oh, my God, my client is going to kill me because I've just proven his guilt to the jury. The judge went back and told the jury to come back tomorrow and we would continue. So I went home. I had to buy a new suit because the blood was all over my pants. My client was yelling at me when we met for court the next morning. I had to go back in front of that jury and complete my closing argument with a bandaged left hand. I had to keep it in my left pocket because I didn't know what to do with it.

"I kept my hand in my pocket the whole time. I held onto the inside of my pocket so I wouldn't make a gesture and pull it out. I finished in about five minutes. I was embarrassed to death. The jury went out and was back in twenty minutes with their verdict. That is normally a good sign for the defense; but, I figured this time it was bad and a slam dunk against my client. My client was still yelling at me, and I apologized to him.

"The judge might declare a mistrial," I said, "but he wants to see what's going to happen first. I figure if the verdict is guilty, he can declare a mistrial. The verdict came back — not guilty. My stomach was ready to burst. The judge looked at them with shock. Not guilty! He said, 'Very well,' and excused the jury.

"At that point, I was beaming like a cat that swallowed the bird. I couldn't believe it. I went outside and waited a little bit for the jury to be released. When they finally appeared, I walked up to the forelady of the jury and told her I was thankful for the verdict. I asked her what it was that caused them to enter a not guilty verdict. Was it my argument? Was it the cross-examination? Was it the charge? She said, 'Well, we figured any lawyer who would cut his hand that badly for his client needs a break.'" And, that's how Willie's first trial ended. Victory over a butter knife.

CHAPTER 14

STATE VS. SMART

*"Accept the challenges so that you may feel
the exhilaration of victory."*

General George S. Patton

Judge Franklin from Toledo appointed Willie to another murder case while Willie was still in Toledo. The defendant looked like Muhammad Ali. The state of Ohio charged the defendant with killing three drug dealers with a shotgun. Willie drove to the murder scene. According to reports, the killer shot three guys in the heads and shoulders. Their brains were literally on the ceiling and parts of their heads blown off. To protect the guilty and for ethical reasons, we'll call the defendant Jim Jones.

Jones' trial would last a week. Willie tried to convince the police to talk to him, but they refused. They would not tell Willie what they knew or what had happened. Willie took some witness statements, but couldn't be sure what their testimony would be. The prosecutor was cagey and didn't have the police testify before the grand jury so Willie was unable to read their testimony. As the trial approached, Willie found himself in the dark.

The prosecution called a Toledo police officer to testify. During the trial it came out that one of the three drug dealers had made a dying declaration to this officer. After being shot in the shoulder and face, with part of his head blown off, he lived long enough to stumble down the steps, open the door, and identify the killer to the police. The prosecution set up the dying declaration as due to apprehension of death.

"What did you physically observe?" asked the prosecution.

"Well, the left side of his face and part of his skull were gone, I could see his brain. He was bleeding profusely."

"Did he have apprehension of death?

"Yes."

The prosecutor did not ask the officer who the dying man had said shot him, ask the officer other details of the victim's dying proclamation.

Willie began to cross-examine the officer. A dying declaration is a powerful piece of evidence and they are admitted on the assumption if a person is about to die and meet his Maker, they won't do so with a lie on their lips. The legal theory is you want to tell the truth. A dying declaration is an exception to the hearsay rule (which prohibits hearsay testimony).

"So I was with the defendant. The prosecutor was setting me up. He wanted me to ask what the dying man said. I assumed the officer would say that the victim told him my defendant had shot him. This was powerful testimony because the police had put Jones at the scene and then running away. They did not have a witness to say Jones shot him. I went back and forth with Jones about what to do, and finally the judge told me to start my questioning," recalls Willie.

"I began my cross-examination of the officer, and had to decide whether or not to ask him, 'What did the dying man tell you?' The trial was going poorly, so I said to the officer, 'Did the dying man give you a declaration?'"

"Yes, he did."

"Did you write down what the man told you, thinking I would have something objective to look at?"

"I did not write it down."

"Now, wait a minute. This is a murder case! This is an important case. You have to put down, as part of your duties, all the evidence that you have in your possession. Why would you not write down what the victim told you about who killed him if he was about to die? Why would you not do that?"

"I'm not required to do that and I didn't do it."

"Don't you think it's your job?"

"I don't think so."

"We went back and forth, with me trying to undermine him in front of the jury, but I wasn't making any headway." Willie said.

"I then said to the officer, 'What did the dying man tell you?' He looked at the jury and clearly stated, 'Larry Jones killed me.' Larry Jones was the brother of Jim Jones. They looked so much alike they could have passed as identical twins. So the other witnesses that put Jim Jones at the scene may have been mistaken. It may have been his brother, Larry.

"I intently questioned the officer. I went through all the stuff to establish details about the victim's condition. What did he look like? Was he conscious? Was he verbal? Did you believe what he told you? I went through everything to establish that the victim knew he was dying. Then I said, 'Who did he say shot him?'

"'Larry Jones shot me,' the officer answered.

"I said, 'Thank you, officer. No other questions.' He left the stand.

"In my closing argument I made a big deal of the death proclamation because why would a dying man lie? Wouldn't anyone in that position want to communicate the truth?

"The jury was out only about a half an hour. They came back and found him not guilty! That was the biggest case I ever had up to that point. About three months later, I was at a department store shopping. I looked across the aisle and saw Jim Jones, my client.

"What are you doing Jim?"

"Ah, can't get work. I'm just doing this and that."

"You not back in business (drugs)?"

"Yeah. I got back in. The money's too easy."

"Jim, let me ask you a question. It is just you and I here and I'd like to know, did you kill those three people? No one can ever use it against you. It would be double jeopardy. I'm your lawyer. Did you kill those people?"

"Yeah, I killed them."

About a year later, Willie returned to Cincinnati to the Hamilton County Public Defender's Office. A lawyer in the prosecutor's office informed Willie that Jim had been killed in a drug deal gone bad. "Justice was done for Jim Jones," Willie said.

CHAPTER 15

LESLIE ISAIAH GAINES

"Age wrinkles the body. Quitting wrinkles the soul."

Douglas MacArthur

When Willie returned to Cincinnati from Toledo he worked in the public defender's office of Hamilton County.

As a public defender, Willie made about $13,000 a year. He tried multiple cases a day and he argued motions. Motions are requests of the court in cases. He worked hard and wasn't making much money. Willie soon noticed an African-American criminal defense attorney in Cincinnati who looked like Frederick Douglass, named Leslie Isaiah Gaines.

"I saw Gaines in court. He was a very impressive lawyer. I walked up to him and said, 'I'd like to work for you,'" said Willie.

"We've never had a white lawyer in the firm before," replied Gaines.

"Well, before you, there was never a black lawyer like you."

"Can you be at the Colony Restaurant tomorrow morning at eight? We have a firm meeting every Wednesday at that time."

"I'll be there."

Willie woke up early and arrived before eight.

"I walked in and there sat Les Gaines, his wife Debbie, James Keys, Michael Edwards and Elsworth Love. All were black. I walked in and sat down and had breakfast with them," Willie said. After breakfast, Willie was in the Gaines firm.

At six foot four and two hundred eighty pounds with a booming voice, Gaines commanded respect when he walked into a room. His voice rivals that of James Earl Jones. The lawyers seated around the table at the Colony dressed to the nines. Willie realized he needed to spruce up his act to conform. He was from the not-so-well-heeled public defender's office. After Gaines hired Willie, they tried many significant cases together in Hamilton County over the next few years.

One warm afternoon in the Gaines law firm office in the Mercantile Library Building in downtown Cincinnati, the air blew through the open windows.

"Mr. Cunningham, I have a call for you," yelled the receptionist.

"Hello, this is Bill Cunningham," as Willie took the call.

"I don't want any niggers representing me. Are you a white lawyer?" asked the voice of prejudice on the other end of the phone.

"Hold on a minute," replied Willie.

Willie put the phone down, climbed out of his chair, and walked down the hall to Les Gaines' office. Gaines sat behind his huge desk with his always-present suspenders strapped across his shirt. His tie was loose and he had his huge arms behind his head and his feet up on his desk.

"Les, we may have a problem here."

"What's the problem, Cousin Willie?"

Les Gaines referred to all of his fellow blacks as his brother. Whites were his cousins.

"I've got this white guy on the phone who just told me he didn't want any niggers representing him."

Willie braced for a recrimination.

"Let me tell you what, Cousin Willie. It matters not the color of a man's skin, but the color of a man's money. Charge him twice as much and take the damn case."

Willie turned around and walked back to his office. He picked up the phone and said:

"I'm your man. Bring me $3,000 tomorrow and I'll represent you."

Willie practiced with Leslie Gaines for three years. Gaines always received fifty percent of whatever Willie made, so Willie began looking for a better deal. He hooked up at a firm, Niehaus & Niehaus, a firm which produced Niehaus judges. Willie actually practiced on his own inside the firm. However, from working with Leslie Gaines, Willie was an experienced trial lawyer and no longer needed a mentor. A young, aspiring criminal defense attorney could not have had a better mentor than Leslie Gaines, who later became a judge in Hamilton County Municipal Court. He left the bench after a few years since he claimed he saw the face of Jesus Christ inside a marble pillar; thereafter Gaines became a man of the cloth.

Chapter 16

"Pay for Africa or Die with Me"

"I know not what course others may take; but as for me, give me liberty, or give me death."

Patrick Henry

Willie served not only as a public defender in state court, but also as a public defender in the Cincinnati federal court system. This meant his name was on a list for federal judges to assign Willie to represent criminal defendants eligible for a court-appointed lawyer. A Judge Porter appointed Willie to represent an African-American man charged with robbing a bank in downtown Cincinnati. It appeared to be an open and shut case for the prosecution.

Willie's new client "allegedly" walked into a bank in downtown Cincinnati and leveled a shotgun at a bank teller. He placed the barrel of the shotgun on the ledge between the customer counter and teller, cocked the shotgun and handed the teller a note written on a bank deposit slip that the robber allegedly had removed from the bank a few days earlier.

The brilliant bank robber, whoever he was, cut words out of a magazine to form the phrase "Pay for Africa or die with me." He cut each word separately out of a magazine so no one could determine they came from one magazine.

"The guy was brilliant," said Willie with a full force of sarcasm.

Whoever the robber was, he used Scotch tape to individually tape to the bank deposit to form the words cut from magazines. He used his bare hands to tape the words. That proved to be an obvious mistake as it left great finger prints.

As the robber held a shotgun two feet from the chest of a teller, security cameras rolled. The teller read the note: "Pay for Africa or die with me." The teller dutifully placed all the money in her drawer in a bag she had behind the counter. She grabbed all the money from her fellow tellers too. She also placed into the bag a hot packet. A hot packet is a packet which looks like a packet of money with a few real bills on top, but inside lies an orange dye which will explode after the robber leaves a bank.

"My client, thinking he had pulled off the heist of the century, left the bank with his loot," Willie related, laughing.

The robber jumped into his car which he illegally parked at Fountain Square on Vine Street. As he drove up Vine Street in his late model car, the packet exploded and a large cloud of orange dye poured out the windows of his car from the satchel of money. He ran red lights as he drove up Vine Street from downtown toward his residence near 25th and Vine.

"Police officers who were walking their beat on that warm summer day observed the car driving at a high rate of speed with orange clouds of dye pouring out all four windows as it sped by them. It was an obvious bank robbery in progress," Willie said.

The police followed him by cruiser and on foot up Vine Street. The robber slammed on the brakes, ran up the steps to a third floor apartment carrying the satchel of money with an orange cloud following him with every step. By the time he reached the apartment, two or three blocks of Vine Street had filled with an orange dye.

As the robber reached his third floor apartment, he entered his bedroom, threw the packet on the bed, jumped into the closet and shut the door. The police were only a minute behind him. They broke in the door and found Willie's client hiding in the closet. The packet and satchel of money were on the bed. The entire apartment was consumed with orange dye.

Willie maintained in his defense that the State really had little evidence of his client's guilt and had nothing upon which to convict him of armed robbery. As all good defense attorneys, he did so with a straight face. At trial, the federal prosecutors brought in an FBI fingerprint expert. Fingerprints are clear indicators of guilt or innocence under most circumstances. Willie's client wanted Willie to reject any admissions, so Willie did not admit to anything on behalf of his client. The prosecutors presented evidence that when the Defendant taped each of the words "Pay for Africa or die with me" on the deposit slip, that his fingerprints were left on each of the pieces of Scotch tape.

"The FBI fingerprint expert from Quantico, Virginia, proved beyond a shadow of a doubt that my client's fingerprints were on the scotch tape that he used on those seven letters. They also had the photographs of my client robbing the bank. They also had the identification of my client from the teller that, in fact, claimed my client was the fellow who robbed the bank. They called numerous police officers who testified they saw a car registered to my client driving up Vine Street with the windows down. They also called the officers who pulled him out of the closet. They recovered the money and the exploding pack. That is all they had in this case. That's all they had!" Willie said.

"I developed this theory that I went about selling to the jury, that, in fact, my client was watching a soap opera in the middle of the afternoon in his apartment when his older brother who looked just like him came running in the front door of the apartment with orange dye trailing him. He asked my client to hide the money, which my client refused to do. He then dropped the money onto the bed, jumped out the window and proceeded down the fire escape, out the back. My client heard a lot of men running upstairs screaming. Thinking he's about to be robbed, he jumped in the closet where he had a sawed-off shotgun already in position for security reasons. He was waiting in the closet and hiding from the desperadoes who were breaking into his apartment."

"In fact, the older brother looked quite a bit like my client, and I had pictures of the older brother. The teller at the bank said it was entirely possible the older brother is the person who held her up because they looked so much alike. The fingerprints on the Scotch tape could easily be explained away because the older brother, who wanted to obviate his own guilt, knew that my client had used the Scotch tape the day before. So he purposely used the Scotch tape with my client's fingerprints on it to put those letters and words on this note, because nobody can be that stupid as to use the Scotch tape in order to convict himself."

Willie was using the "stupidest defense" in the inverse. It was not that his client was stupid. It was that his client could not be so stupid as to do that. Judge Porter, during long deliberations when the jury was out, said that in his thirty-year federal career he had never admonished a jury in open court ever before, but if this jury found this guy not guilty, he was going to do it in open court. After two or three days of deliberations, they found him not guilty of bank robbery, but guilty of possessing the weapon that was next to him in the closet.

"This jury thought the evidence was so obvious that it could not be the truth. I came up with some scenarios in my argument from Perry Mason and from Owen Marshall, television lawyers, that nobody could have been so stupid as to commit a crime and tape their own fingerprints. They bought it because they were looking for the real story there," explains Willie.

Willie's client never explained to him why the note said, "Pay for Africa or die."

"I assume it was because he was an African-American seeking reparation," Willie says.

CHAPTER 17

A FINAL TRIAL

*"Of all the properties which belong to honorable men,
not one is so highly prized as that of character."*

Henry Clay

The year 1998 would see Willie's last murder case. It would be in Judge Ralph Winkler's courtroom in Hamilton County, Ohio. Willie believes it was Judge Winkler's last case before the Honorable Judge moved up to the Court of Appeals. The Winklers can boast of the father being a Court of Appeals Judge and two of his sons being Hamilton County Common Pleas Judge.

One of Willie's restaurant employees had a brother charged with bludgeoning a prostitute to death in the Over-the-Rhine area of downtown Cincinnati. The accused lived next door to the victim. He was white and she was black. Willie had not tried a case in many years. He first spoke to his client in jail. Willie could not get him released on bond of $25,000 because Judge Winkler was tough and he would not lower it.

The prosecution had the benefit of an eyewitness to the murder. This witness would testify that William Donovan committed the murder. Donovan also confessed to the murder to a cellmate.

"I figure all they had was an eyewitness and a confession. How hard is that case? I said, no problem at all," laughs Willie.

Willie took the case as a self-test to see if he still had what it took. It did not look like a murder case he could win, because of the eyewitness and the confession. Willie hung out in a few bars in the rough Over-the-Rhine section of Cincinnati where this eye-witness hung out. He also hired a detective to tail the woman who was the eyewitness. Willie knew he had to destroy the eyewitness and then destroy the confession to the cellmate. All good lawyers know legwork can make the difference.

Willie's private detective, who wired himself, was David Cul-breth. He used to be a Channel 19 weatherman. Channel 19 is a local television station in Cincinnati. Culbreth wired himself up and visited a bar one night where the witness was hanging out. She was a black female whose nickname was the "Snake." She was drinking at the bar. Culbreth did not buy her drinks, but he sat down next to the Snake. He began talking to Snake about what was going on and got her talking about the murder. She said on tape that she really didn't see anything that night, but she had some charges against her and she wanted the police to give her a break. She told the police officers what they wanted to hear and then they would give her a break on her cases. Willie secured all this on tape. Willie then requested the medical records of the cell-mate who happened to be suffering from paranoid delusional schizophrenia. One of components of this disease is that one is unable to perceive reality correctly.

"So I figured I had the confession in a pretty good shape, and I had the eyewitness compromised. I didn't file any discovery requests with the State because if you do, they send you back discovery requests. I did not want them to know who my witnesses were. I didn't want them to know that David Culbreth had a tape. I did not want them to know I had a shrink who was going to call this guy a liar. So the prosecutor thought that I had been out of touch, that I didn't know what I was doing, and I hadn't tried a case in a while."

"So the trial began and I spoke to the prosecutor," Willie began.

"Well, you never filed a discovery request, Bill," the judge replied.

"Oh, man, I'm sorry, I forgot!"

"That's okay," the judge said. Willie was surprised and thankful.

"Who are your witnesses?" Willie inquired.

"Who are your witnesses going to be?" the prosecutor asked.

Willie hedged, but not enough to make the prosecutor suspicious, then he "confessed" that he simply wasn't sure how he would proceed.

"Well, who you got?" the prosecutor asked again.

"I'm not sure yet."

"So she thought I had blundered in not filing discovery requests. But in reality, I was setting her up. Then the witness, Snake, took the stand; she was about thirty, a skinny African-American drug abuser."

"They call her the Snake for obvious reasons. She goes through the direct examination with the prosecutor clean as a hound's tooth. She claims she was in the room with her roommate's girl-friend, and then went next door. She testified that she heard an argument, yelling and screaming. She heard blood-curdling cries. She cracked open the door and saw my client with a shovel, blud-geoning her friend to death against a pillow. She testified she dialed 911 and she ran out of the house," Willie said. "Then I began to cross-examine her: "You've just testified under oath to this jury that you witnessed this murder. Were you in a position to see the murder?"

"Yes."

"You're under oath, and you know what an oath means?"

"Yes."

"Do you understand this is a serious matter?"

"Yes, I do."

"You wouldn't lie to this jury, would you?"

"No."

"These twelve people have taken time from their lives to come down here; do you understand how important this is?"

"Yes, I do."

"And you loved your roommate?"

"Yes, I did."

"Isn't it true that you never did see anything that night?"

"Mr. Cunningham, that is a lie. I saw it all."

Then Willie brought out his tape recorder, and asked, "Isn't it true you were sitting at the Bayhorse Inn in downtown Cincinnati at or near nine p.m. on such a date, next to a person named David Culbreth?"

Suddenly the woman went from arrogant and smug to scared.

"Well, I might have," she replied.

"Then Willie went through some more questions to set her up. And then he began reading from the transcript he had made of the audiotape. Didn't you say this? Didn't you say that?"

"Well, you've got the tape, you probably know it," she said.

"You lied, didn't you?"

"Well, yeah, I did lie," she admitted.

"So the jurors, who had been staring at my client, began staring at her. They could not believe what was going on. Then I brought in the doctor who said that the cellmate who got the confession was delusional.

"I also did something else. My son Evan was about twenty-four years old. And I asked the judge for permission to have him sit at the counsel table with me to help me. He was going to college and might be a lawyer. The judge allowed it. I put my son between me and this alleged murderer, thinking in my mind that the jurors would be thinking, would Cunningham put his own son next to the murderer if he believed the guy is a murderer? I told Evan, that during breaks he should be animated with this guy, talk with him. I told my client to talk to my son, talk to me, stand up, look at the jury, and smile. Eye contact is important. I set up the trial that way.

"So the jury was out for a day and came back with a not guilty verdict. During the time the jury was out I asked Judge Winkler, 'What would you have done if I had tried this to the bench?'"

"And he said, 'I would have convicted him in a heartbeat. They had other evidence such as blood splatter evidence and they had found the shovel.'

"The jury came back and found him not guilty. About a week later, I received a letter from a person on the jury claiming they hadn't wanted to believe the Snake, but they liked the fact that my son was sitting next to the murderer because no father would put his son close to a murderer! And if I thought he was innocent and there was evidence to indicate that, that was good enough for them, if Bill Cunningham, Mr. Law and Order, thought the guy was innocent, that was good enough for them.

I felt so guilty after that, I never tried another jury case."

"As the client was being led out of the Hamilton County Justice Center, I said, 'Let me ask you something. Did you kill that woman? I'd like to know.'"

"Yeah, I killed her."

COURT OF COMMON PLEAS
HAMILTON COUNTY, OHIO

THE STATE OF OHIO	:	**CASE NO. B-9709432**
Plaintiff	:	
	:	
-v-	:	**JUDGE RALPH WINKLER**
	:	
WILLIAM C. DONOVAN	:	
	:	
Defendant	:	<u>**NOT GUILTY VERDICT**</u>

We, the Jury, in the issue joined, find the Defendant, WILLIAM C.

DONOVAN, NOT GUILTY OF MURDER, 2903.02(A) R.C.,

as charged in the Indictment.

1. _[signature]_   7. _Mary Spradlin_
2. _Wesley P. Leazard_   8. _Lila Rosenbloom_
3. _[signature]_   9. _[signature] Hopkins_
4. _Ann Tracy Arand_   10. _Donna M. Tellent_
5. _Marcia Hellmeyer_ 11. _Virginia Fisher_
6. _Wanda Hollbrook_ 12. _Robert J. Mayne_
                                      Foreperson

March 2, 1998
[signature]

"Okay," I said, "I appreciate your telling me the truth."

About six months later, Willie's client was found dead in Over-the-Rhine, frozen to death. He drank himself into a stupor, fell out of a bar, tried to get home in subzero temperatures, fell into a snowbank and was not discovered until the next morning, and he froze to death. Justice was done again.

Willie served two teams as the President of the Ohio State Bar Young Lawyers Division. Since 1978, there is the William D. Cunningham Outstanding Young Lawyer award, which was given by the Ohio State Bar to an outstanding young lawyer in the State of Ohio. He won the award before it was named for him.

CHAPTER 18

ALAN BROWNING

*"Living in dreams of yesterday, we find ourselves
still dreaming of impossible future conquests."*

Charles Lindbergh

*I*n 1978 and 1979, Willie represented, along with Leslie
Gaines, four cop killers who killed five police officers. Over
a year and a half, Gaines was Johnny Cochran, and Willie was
Carl Douglas, except Willie would never have a hit like *Kung Fu
Fighting*. Gaines and Willie tried the cases to juries. In Cincinnati,
where cop killers are quite rare, that was a seminal moment.
During the middle of these killings, all the Cincinnati police
officers drove their cruisers to City Hall, filled the streets with
their police cars, turned on the sirens, snapped the ignition keys
off in the ignition and locked the doors. The officers, in their
uniforms, and their families marched on City Hall. Inside City
Hall, the officers demanded better uniforms, better weapons and
more support from City Council. Les Gaines and Willie attended
one of those meetings.

"We had to walk through a crowd of in-uniform cops and their
wives who were outraged that Les Gaines and I were representing
the cop killers and City Council for not doing enough to protect
their husbands from death," explained Willie.

The black community, on the other hand, considered it racism
to suggest black men were responsible for the murder of white officers.

"I believe in the last fifty years in the City of Cincinnati every cop killer has been black, and all but one or two cops killed have been white. So Les Gaines, being black, and me being white, were able to walk that line. Les could placate the blacks and I could speak to the whites," explains Willie.

No overall riot took place, but there were numerous cases of "blue flu." It cost thousands of dollars to fix the police cruisers. The city went unprotected for a while, because the officers demanded stress leave.

In the middle of this turmoil, a radio talk show host named Alan Browning on 55 WKRC in Cincinnati asked Willie to come on his talk show to publicly answer and explain to the public how a young lawyer could represent anyone who killed a police officer. Browning was the dominant radio personality in Greater Cincinnati for many years. Alan thought Willie was a solid guest, so he invited Willie back once a month to do "Ask The Attorney."Willie would go on the air once a month and answer general legal questions. The by-product of these appearances resulted in the growth of Willie's practice. Willie received an avalanche of calls from people who wanted representation on divorces, wills and criminal cases. Willie would be a regular on the Alan Browning show once a month for four years. At age thirty one, Willie was on his way to the top of his legal profession, not the radio business.

At that time, the program director of 55 WKRC was the legendary Randy Michaels. His real name, according to Willie, was Ben Homel. Michaels put together 230 radio stations under a company called Jacor Broadcasting. In 1999, he sold Jacor to Clear Channel for $3.8 billion. He then became CEO of Clear Channel in 2002. He would later become the COO of the Tribune Company.

In the summer of 1983, Randy Michaels left 55 WKRC. With a small investor group he purchased 700WLW. Michaels called Willie in July of 1983, and, because Willie performed a little legal work for Alan Browning, informed Willie of his desire to hire Alan Browning when Browning's contract expired at 55 WKRC. Michaels wanted to hire Alan to do the evening talk show on 700WLW.

Alan Browning was a late-night radio talk show host. He did a show called "Desperate & Dateless" which became his claim to fame. He had men calling on one line and women calling on another. He would hook them up to go out on dates. Willie told Alan of his call from Randy Michaels. Alan and Randy were also friends. Willie informed Alan of Randy's desire to hire him to work at 700WLW. Based upon 700WLW being a larger station and the fact that he liked Randy, Alan told Willie to negotiate a deal which would land Alan Browning at 700WLW.

Over the next two weeks, Willie and Randy met in a Perkins Pancake House and other places working out a deal where Alan Browning would leave 55 WKRC in August. At that time, WLW had lower ratings than WKRC.

"WKRC was a powerhouse. WLW was in the crapper. But WLW had the signal and WKRC had the personalities," explains Willie. Near the end of the negotiations, Willie saw Alan Browning almost every day. Willie suggested to Alan they go back to Harold Calvin, Alan's boss at WKRC and "play tennis to obtain the best possible deal." Since they were talking to Randy Michaels, who had just left, and Calvin and Michaels were at odds with each other, Willie believed he could squeeze more money out of WKRC.

Alan Browning rebuffed the suggestion. "I want to work for Randy. I want to work at 700. It's not about the money. A few bucks are not going to make any difference. I want to work for the Big One," Alan Browning said to Willie. After the deal was made, it was announced on a Friday in August of 1983. It was in the local daily newspapers, the *Cincinnati Enquirer* and the *Cincinnati Post*.

"It was in the paper. That was like a coup for Randy Michaels. He was in his thirties. He would go on to help put together the largest radio company in the world, Clear Channel. But at that point, he was just in Cincinnati, Ohio," explains Willie.

The deal was announced on a Friday. That afternoon, Willie walked into 700WLW for the very first time. It was located on 3 East Fourth Street in downtown Cincinnati. Willie walked two steps behind Alan Browning and Randy Michaels. Alan was the star. Willie "carried his briefcase." Willie met Bob Trumpy,

Gary Burbank, and the other stars of the radio station. Michaels introduced Alan and added "Oh, this is Bill Cunningham back here." Willie walked around and looked at the station with curiosity, but he was a mere afterthought to everyone in the room. Willie had listened to Cincinnati Reds games on 700WLW but little else; he never listened to talk radio.

CHAPTER 19

WILLIE'S OPPORTUNITY

"Think of yourself as on the threshold of unparalleled
success. A whole, clear, glorious life lies before you.
Achieve! Achieve!"

Andrew Carnegie

*A*lan Browning was scheduled to begin his 700WLW career the following Monday at nine p.m. He would be on air from nine p.m. to one a.m. He was working eight p.m. to twelve a.m. at WKRC. Willie lay on his couch at home the day of the planned Alan Browning debut on 700WLW, and he received a call from Randy Michaels a little after eight on the scheduled Monday night. Randy began the call with a diatribe of cursing.

"Randy, I can't understand you. What's wrong?" Willie asked.

"That damn Alan Browning is on the air at 55 WKRC right now! What's the bastard going to do, get in his car and drive to 700WLW. You son of a bitch!"

"Randy, calm down. I have no idea."

"Are you a part of this?"

"I'm not part of anything. I don't know what you're talking about."

Willie ran over to a radio and turned it on. He tuned to 55 WKRC and sure enough, at 8:10 p.m., Alan Browning's voice was on 55 WKRC. "Holy crap!" Willie said to himself.

"Bill, you call that bastard and find out what the hell's going on," Randy screamed as Willie returned to the phone.

At the 8:20 commercial break, Willie called Alan on the 55 WKRC hotline. "Alan, what the hell are you doing? Are you going to drive over before 9:00 to WLW?"

"No. I changed my mind."

"You changed your mind? You signed a contract! It's in the damn newspaper!"

"Get me out of the contract."

"I'm not getting you out of the contract. Why didn't you call me?"

"Well, I felt embarrassed about it."

"You don't call your lawyer?"

"No, I got another lawyer. I spoke to 55 WKRC and I signed a better deal."

"You son of a bitch! You bastard! You can't do that to me! Why would you do that to Randy? It makes me look like shit!"

"I don't care. Get me out of the contract."

"Bullshit! You get your other lawyer to get you out of the contract. I'm done with you!"

Willie hung up the phone in anger and embarrassed disbelief. At 8:30, and with great trepidation, he called Randy Michaels back.

"Randy, I've got some bad news for you."

Willie told Randy about his conversation with Alan and Randy went nuts again.

"I'm suing his ass! I've had it with him. I'll tell you what, meet me down there at 9:00."

"Me?"

"We will do free legal advice at 9:00."

Willie, being finished with Alan Browning, jumped in his car, drove fast and made it to the WLW radio station at exactly 9:01. The news would be over at 9:06 and there would be no one behind the microphone.

"Where's Randy?" Willie asked the board operator, Dave Armsbruster.

"I don't know. He'll be here."

9:06 arrived. No Randy. Willie had been a guest on Alan

Browning's show, but he had never hosted a show. Willie, under the circumstances, walked in the studio to wing a show.

"I went on the air and told everyone I had no idea what I was doing." He said, "I've never done this before by myself. You've heard me on 55 WKRC. I did a talk show about legal advice. Call in and I'll give you legal advice," explains Willie.

At 10:00 p.m., Randy called Willie off the air.

"Randy, where in the hell are you? You've hung me out to dry."

"No. I didn't. I wanted to see if you could do it by yourself."

"Well, thanks a lot."

So, for the next eight months, until April 1984, Willie did a talk show five nights a week from 9:00 p.m. to 1:00 a.m., had a very active law practice with 40-50 criminal cases. He also coached his son's basketball and baseball teams. Willie was a very busy man, and Willie the radio talk show host was launched.

CHAPTER 20

A RADIO FUTURE?

*"Obstacles are those frightful things you see
when you take your eyes off your goal."*

Henry Ford

R andy Michaels began his radio career as an engineer. He
also did some on-air work. At one point, he worked at five
different stations under three different names. In the early 1970s,
he became Taft Broadcasting's Vice President of Programming.
In 1983, with a partner, Robert Lawrence, he formed Seven Hills
Broadcasting. WLW was one of the stations he bought. In 1986,
Seven Hills merged with Jacor.

In 1992, Michaels hired a young Sean Hannity to join Jacor as a
talk show host in Atlanta. Sean Hannity is the well-known national radio and television host, author and champion of conservative
political principles. He hosts a radio show, *The Sean Hannity Show*
from WABC (AM) in New York and Fox News' *Hannity's America*
and *Hannity* daily at 9:00 p.m. on FOX.

Hannity hosted his first talk show in 1989 at the volunteer college station at University of California Santa Barbara, KCSB-FM.
KCSB canceled his show over a charge Hannity discriminated
against gays and lesbians. He could have returned after KCSB re-
versed their decision due in part, of all things, the support of the
Santa Barbara Chapter of the ACLU.

Hannity placed an ad in radio publications saying he was "the
most talked about college radio host in America" and WVNN in

Athens, Alabama, hired him to be the afternoon talk show host. In 1992, he moved to WGST in Atlanta. In September 1996, Fox News hired him to co-host the television program *Hannity & Colmes* with Alan Colmes, now replaced by *Hannity*.

In 1997, Randy Michaels cut a deal with Rush Limbaugh. Rush is the number one radio talk show host in the country. *The Rush Limbaugh Show* is nationally syndicated and airs on Premiere Radio Networks throughout the world. He has been considered the savior of AM radio. In a 1993 cover story, the National Review called him "The Leader of the Opposition" to the Clinton presidency.

After college, Rush was actually a Top 40 music radio disc jockey on station WIXZ in the Pittsburgh area. He once used the name Jeff Christie as a call name. That was on WKQV in 1972. After jumping around several radio stations, Rush settled in Kansas City, Missouri. He became director of promotions with the Kansas City Royals after taking a break from radio.

In 1984, Rush returned to radio and the talk show business at KFBK in Sacramento, California. He actually replaced Morton Downey, Jr. on the station. After the 1987 repeal of the Fairness Doctrine, Rush moved to New York in 1988 to begin his national radio show.

Rush's show on WABC, 770 AM had a great debut in its timing. It was between the Democratic and Republican 1988 Presidential Conventions. In May 1999, Sam Zell and Randy Michaels merged Jacor with Clear Channel Communications. In three years, Clear Channel grew from 425 to 1200 stations. Michaels remained CEO until July 2002.

In April 1984, while Willie continued radio, John Socko Wiethe, chairman of the Democrat Party in Hamilton County, asked Willie to run against Common Pleas Court Judge Robert Kraft.

At the time, Willie also served as an assistant attorney general for the State of Ohio in insanity hearings. It's difficult not to find humor that the "Great American" handled insanity hearings.

"It was kind of part of the deal. If you're an AG and you're a Democrat, and Socko Wiethe, a living legend in football and basketball and Chairman of the Democratic Party for thirty years, asked you to do something, you did it," laughs Willie.

After the request by Wiethe, Willie decided to discuss the idea with Randy Michaels. At the time, Willie made $12,000 a year for his radio gig.

"Randy, I want to know if I have a future in radio," Willie said.

"Why do you ask?"

"I've been doing it for eight months and I don't get any feedback at all. I come in here at 8:45 at night. I leave at one. I never see anybody. I don't know how I'm doing. Do I have a future in radio?"

"No, Willie, I don't think you do," Randy replied. "I don't think you're going to make it."

"Well, I appreciate the honesty because I can run for Judge. I can practice law more, and frankly, I don't think I was very good anyway."

At that time, the Fairness Doctrine was in effect. The Fairness Doctrine was a United States FCC Regulation requiring broadcast licenses to prevent controversial issues of public importance in a matter deemed by the FCC to be honest, equitable, and balanced. The FCC has since withdrawn the doctrine, and the courts questioned certain aspects of the doctrine. There is a fear it will be revived.

That meant Willie did shows such as "Petunias — How to Raise Flowers," legal advice, fixing cars, self-help shows, had doctors and accountants as guests and produced all types of advice shows.

"If you put a political issue on the air, you had to offer equal time to somebody with a different political viewpoint who may not have radio skills," Willie explained. "Therefore, you didn't do political shows."

If there were five political viewpoints and the Federal Communication Commission took a complaint from anybody, it would begin a process of investigating whether the host allowed all viewpoints. Radio had a rule — do not talk about politics during talk radio because it would not be possible to cover all the areas.

Willie met again with Socko Wiethe to inform him he could run for Judge. Then Willie changed his mind.

"I thought about it some more and decided I didn't want to run for Judge because if I ran for Judge, I couldn't be in the AG's office. I enjoyed practicing law. I couldn't beat Kraft anyway because he was a very popular Republican judge," said Willie.

So, Willie returned to Randy Michaels to continue his radio gig until further notice.

"Randy, I'd like to keep doing radio," he said.

"Willie, I've got a person I'm going to interview for the job," Randy replied. "Can you do it for two more weeks?"

"Sure, I'll do it for two more weeks."

The Chicago prospect Michaels had in mind to replace Willie came to Cincinnati and left without accepting the position. Randy Michaels then asked Willie to handle the show for two or three more weeks.

The bottom line — Willie's entire radio career was an accident. Then, out of the news, and out of Cincinnati, came a financial scandal, which would lift Willie higher in the talk show radio world.

CHAPTER 21

SAVINGS & LOAN CRISIS & MORE

"The three great essentials to achieve anything worthwhile are, first, hard work; second, stick-to-itiveness; third, common sense."

Thomas Edison

*I*n the 1980s and 1990s, more than a thousand savings and loan institutions failed. The ultimate estimated cost was $160 billion. The U.S. government and taxpayers paid $124 billion of the tab. Compared to today's economic crisis and bailouts, this seems mild.

The financial disaster had its origins in Ohio. In March 1985, Cincinnati, Ohio-based Home State Savings Bank was about to collapse. Dick Celeste, Ohio's Governor, declared a bank holiday to avoid a run on the deposits. Celeste also ordered the closure of all state savings and loans. If a savings and loan qualified for membership to the Federal Deposit Insurance Corporation, they could reopen. The claims from Ohio's depositors emptied the state's deposit insurance fund.

Marvin Warner, from Home State, became the face of the savings and loan scandal. He graduated from the University of Alabama with business and law degrees. He served in the U.S. Army during World War II. He became a developer after the war in Birmingham. He served as the United States Ambassador to Switzerland from 1977 to 1979. He owned his hometown Birmingham Stallions during the USFL from 1982-1985. He moved to Cincinnati in 1951. He developed the residential developments of Forest Park and Highland Towers. In 1973, Warner bought Home State Savings Bank. By 1985, Home State had over thirty branches when the bottom fell out. Home State invested $140 million in ESM Government Securities, a Florida company which filed bankruptcy.

A jury convicted Marvin Warner on six counts of fraud for making investments without board approval and three counts of securities violations. Sentenced to ten years in prison, he served less than three. He paid $16 million as a settlement of the $22 million ordered by the Court.

After leaving prison, Warner lived on his 150-acre horse farm in Ocala, Florida. Florida protects a debtor's home under their homestead law. Warner died in 2002 at the age of 82. The University of Alabama Law School still awards a Marvin L. Warner scholarship.

In the summer of 1984, in Cincinnati when Home State Savings & Loan collapsed, depositors lined up to withdraw their money from the bank. The Ohio Deposit Guarantee Fund was bankrupt. Marvin Warner and his partner in crime, Burton Vanguard, were looting their savings & loan and everyone else was losing money. Willie understood the issue. He did a series of radio shows about people losing their money in savings and loans and how savings and loans were in a crisis.

"I began building up my sea legs. I began doing shows that were must-listen-to radio. I emceed events with a group of depositors involving tens of thousands of people. I spoke at the Schmidt Fieldhouse at Xavier. Suddenly, I began doing very well at talk radio. After about six more months, Randy Michaels informed me the best decision he made was hiring me. I reminded him he wanted to fire me," laughs Willie.

On January 28, 1986, the American space shuttle *Challenger* exploded. Willie uses this speech as an example of President Ronald Reagan's greatness. It's worth giving the full text:

Ladies and gentlemen, I'd planned to speak to you tonight to report on the state of the union, but the events of earlier today have led me to change those plans. Today is a day for mourning and remembering. Nancy and I are pained to the core by the tragedy of the shuttle *Challenger*. We know we share this pain with all of the people of our country. This is truly a national loss.

Nineteen years ago, almost to the day, we lost three astronauts in a terrible accident on the ground. But we've never lost an astronaut in flight; we've never had a tragedy like this. And perhaps we've forgotten the courage it took for the crew of the shuttle; but they, the *Challenger* seven, were aware of the dangers, but overcame them and did their jobs brilliantly. We mourn seven heroes: Michael Smith, Dick Scobee, Judith Resnik, Ronald McNair, Ellison Onizuka, Gregory Jarvis, and Christa McAuliffe. We mourn their loss as a nation together.

For the families of the seven, we cannot bear, as you do, the full impact of their tragedy. But we feel the loss, and we're thinking about you so very much. Your loved ones were daring and brave, and they had special grace, that special spirit that says, "Give me a challenge, and I'll meet it with joy." They had a hunger to explore the universe and discover its truths. They wished to serve, and they did. They served all of us.

We've grown used to wonders in this county. It's hard to dazzle us. But for 25 years the United States space program has been doing just that. We've grown used to the idea of space, and perhaps we forget that we've only just begun. We're still pioneers. They, the members of the *Challenger* crew, were pioneers.

And I want to say something to the school children of America who were watching the live coverage of the shuttle's takeoff. I know it's hard to understand, but sometimes painful things like this happen. It's all a part of the process of exploration and discovery. It's all part of taking a chance and expanding a man's horizons. The future doesn't belong to the fainthearted; it belongs to the brave. The *Challenger* crew was pulling us into the future, and we'll continue to follow them.

I've always had great faith in and respect for our space program, and what happened today does nothing to diminish it. We don't hide our space program. We don't keep secrets and cover things up. We do it all up front and public. That is the way freedom is, and we would not change it for a minute. We will continue our quest in space. There will be more shuttle flights and more shuttle crews and yes, more volunteers, more civilians, more teachers in space. Nothing ends here; our hopes and our journeys continue.

I want to add that I wish I could talk to every man and woman who works for NASA or who worked on this mission and tell them: "Your dedication and professionalism have moved and impressed us for decades. And we know of your anguish. We share it."

There's a coincidence today. On this day 390 years ago, the great explorer Sir Francis Drake died aboard ship off the coast of Panama. In his lifetime the great frontiers were the oceans, and a historian later said, "He lived by the sea, died on it, and was buried in it." Well, today we can say of the *Challenger* crew; their dedication was, like Drake's, complete.

The crew of the space shuttle *Challenger* honored us by the manner in which they lived their lives. We will never forget them, nor the last time we saw them, this morning, as they prepared for their journey and waved good-bye and "slipped the surly bonds of earth" to "touch the face of God."

The discussion of the tragedy had talk radio taking off. Within five years, Willie doubled Alan Browning's ratings.

"I drove him out of talk radio because he couldn't compete

against me. I think he's now selling cars in Lima, Ohio," Willie said.

Then in 1988, Congress repealed the Fairness Doctrine. The result — Willie could talk about politics. And, he did more and more. In 1991, the Gulf War provided plenty of material. The war was a conflict between Iraq and a coalition force from thirty-four nations authorized by the United Nations (UN) and led primarily by the United States in order to return Kuwait to the control of the Emir of Kuwait. The conflict developed in the context of the Iran-Iraq War and in 1990 Iraq accused Kuwait of stealing Iraq's oil through slant drilling. The invasion of Kuwait by Iraqi troops was met with immediate economic sanctions against Iraq by some members of the UN Security Council, and with immediate preparation for war by the United States of America and the United Kingdom. The expulsion of Iraqi troops from Kuwait began in January 1991 and was a decisive victory for the coalition forces, which took over Kuwait.

Operation Desert Storm was the U.S. name of the air and land operations and is often used to refer to the conflict. George Bush, #41, had ratings through the roof at the conclusion of the war. However, a souring economy and Bush's reneging on his "no new taxes" pledge would cost him his reelection.

The war was a boom for talk radio. But, even better talk radio would come in the form of Bill Clinton. He was the third-youngest president, just older than Theodore Roosevelt and John F. Kennedy. He became president at the end of the Cold War. He was the first Baby Boomer president. He is the husband of New York Senator, 2008 Democratic presidential candidate and now Secretary of State, Hillary Rodham Clinton.

Clinton was described as a New Democrat. His policies, on issues such as the North American Free Trade Agreement and welfare reform, have been described as "centrist." Clinton presided over the longest period of peacetime economic expansion in American history, which included a balanced budget and a reported federal surplus. Based on congressional accounting rules, at the end of his presidency Clinton reported a surplus of $559 billion. On the heels of a failed attempt at health care reform with a Democratic Congress, for the first time in four years, Republicans won control of the House of Representatives. In his second term, he was impeached by the U.S. House for perjury and obstruction of justice, but was subsequently acquitted by the United States Senate and completed his term.

The Paula Jones and Monica Lewinsky incidents stained his entire Presidency. They fueled conservative talk radio.

"In 1992, Clinton won. For the next eight years, it was wonderful for talk radio. Those were the halcyon days because we had something to fight against," explains Willie.

Clinton did for Willie and talk radio what mustard does for a hotdog.

CHAPTER 22

WILLIE'S STYLE

*I*n the 2008 Holiday Issue of the *Cincinnati* magazine, *Cincinnati Gentlemen*, Willie appeared on the cover in an Uncle Sam costume. The headline on the cover: "Who In the Hell Does Bill Cunningham Think He Is?" Greg Hoard, the Editor-In-Chief, interviewed Willie. They began the story with - "like it or not, Bill Cunningham is the most influential member of the media in the Tri-state area."

I'll put Willie's wit, intelligence and brain up against anyone on national radio. In candor, it's superior. When you have the life experience of being a trial lawyer and a businessman, you have ability, brain and experiences which give you a perspective outside the "professional" talk show host who has never worked outside radio.

Willie's style is different from all the others. He just doesn't do the "conservative talk show" thing; he's an entertainer. He was entertaining on the radio with irreverence long before Jon Stewart and Stephen Colbert were doing so on television. He has style and substance. He has a self-deprecating sense of humor and doesn't take himself too seriously.

Like all hosts, Willie has his very own catchphrases. They are sprinkled throughout his show. The following is an unexhausted list:

- "You're a Great American."
- "I'm the Conscience of America."

- "Let's now go to the American people whom I have loved so well and served so long."
- "Give me a full report."
- "Let's continue now."
- "Average schlepf like me."
- "You're an idiot."
- "Nah, Baby Nah."
- "Let's pick up the pieces."
- "How we looking? Not good." (From Cincinnati Reds broadcaster Marty Brennaman)
- "Where are you now, if anywhere."
- "Truth to power."
- "Your good friend _____" (Sarcastically)
- "I'm a grateful American."
- "I went to Xavier when gay meant you were happy, when Ayds was an appetite suppressant, crack was a deficiency in the sidewalk, and pot was something you cooked in."
- "Liberals have captured America. Conservatives are voices in the wilderness."
- "I changed when it became the party of Jane Fonda."
- "All terrorists are Muslims, not all Muslims are terrorists."
- "If you got big boobies, don't golf."
- "If you want peace, prepare for war."

Willie has advocated the National Underground Railroad Freedom Center be turned into a casino. With respect to Andrea Yates, the mother from Houston found not guilty due to insanity who drowned her five children: She should be drowned.

Willie bets hot fudge sundaes to those will take his bets.

He concludes interviews with guests: "Do you have any questions for me?"

Willie loves matching wits with the "far left" callers because he believes they are unarmed. Many try to get him in trouble by sending nasty emails to Darryl Parks, the program director. Willie does love a good caller. That means someone who has a good take on something or who is so stupid it makes good entertainment.

Blogging in this interactive age is promoted by 700WLW. Willie receives the luxury of one of station's young producers shooting a video message to him during a break in his show. The video blog is posted daily. He does not have to write anything, he just blogs a sixty second message by videotape. You can visit the website and view them at 700WLW.com. As always, they mix humor and news and are thoroughly entertaining. In fact, they are laugh-out-loud funny.

CHAPTER 23

WLW RADIO TEAM

The talk show lineup for WLW is second to none. There is a reason why they dominate the Arbition ratings in every time slot in Cincinnati.

Beginning at 5:00 a.m. to 9:00 p.m. weekday mornings is the venerable Jim Scott. The "elder statesman" of the team, Jim Scott has been a force and the voice on AM Cincinnati radio for decades. Bright and affable, Jim Scott's trademarks are not only wit and courtesy to callers; his show is seamless. There are never any pauses or blips as he transfers from callers, to reports, to analysis to news. He is as smooth as they come on talk radio. His show focuses on news and weather for the morning drive. Jim is the ringmaster and the table setter for all that lies ahead that day.

Following Jim Scott is Mike McConnell. From 9:00 a.m. to noon, Mike gives it "straight up" like a drink on the rocks. Common sense, intolerant, straight forward and always intellectually sarcastic, Mike has little time for boneheads who call in. He covers topical issues from politics to life. He has featured guests and book reviews too.

Willie follows McConnell *after* the National Anthem at high noon. This is very appropriate for the Great American. He begins every show with George Thorogood's, "Bad to the Bone."

After Willie from 3:00 p.m. to 6:00 p.m. for drive time is the "dynamic duo" of Tracy Jones and Eddie Fingers. It's marketed as *The View* for men. Tracy Jones, a former major leaguer, including with the Cincinnati Reds, did *Inside Baseball* on weekends for a decade on 700WLW. Eddie Fingers is an icon in Cincinnati as the former morning rock and roller on Clear Channel's sister station — WEBN. He played the records and entertained for decades at WEBN, the #1 rock station in Cincinnati forever. Eddie is really the "straight man" to Tracy's satire. Tracy entertains by purposely saying the darnedest things like a contestant on Art Linkletter's old show. What is most remarkable is the audience thinks he is serious.

After drive time is Lance McAlister who is the *Sports Talk* man from 6-9 p.m. He receives the honor of having to talk about the hapless Reds and the pathetic Cincinnati Bengals.

Following McAlister is Scott Sloan. The youngster in the group; he not only talks about topics which nine to midnight listeners will find entertaining; he's also the most active blogger of the group. As he likes to say, he's a hit with the "perverts." His blog ranges from racy to mild. His theme song is Green Day's *(I Don't Want to Be An) American Idiot.*

From midnight to 5:00 a.m. is the Bubba Bo or Steve Summers, rotating on the American Trucking Network. From coast to coast, truckers tune in and call in to discuss every issue affecting truckers and their industry.

On weekends, there is Gary Jeff Walker from 5:30-9:00 a.m. From 9:00-11:00 a.m. is Dangerous "Darryl Parks," the program director. From 11:00-12:00 is the most boring show on radio. They must pay Clear Channel *a lot* of money. It's the national Mutual Fund Show.

The rest of the weekend is usually *Sports Talk, Weekends with Mike McConnell* and the "Best of" whatever they choose to replay. Bengals, Reds, Cincinnati Bearcats, and Xavier Musketeers sports always have the air when they play.

Jeff Henderson heads up the news team. His band of reporters — Bill Rinehart, Brian Combs, Bill Bangert, Chuck Ingram, Jack Crumley, Brant Schulz, Brandi Srader, Tim Lewis and Terry Lafferty — report traffic, news, weather and sports on the tens at morning and afternoon drive time.

CHAPTER 24

THE RADIO GAME

"In the middle of difficulty lies opportunity."

Albert Einstein

*D*arryl Parks is the current Director of AM Operations at Clear Channel Radio in Cincinnati, Ohio. It's a position he's held for nine years. He's Willie's radio boss. Darryl Parks first heard Willie on the radio while Darryl worked in Kokomo, Indiana. "I was working in Kokomo and in Indianapolis. It was the mid-eighties and WLW was transforming into a news talk station at that time. I caught a buzz. I kind of knew something was going on. That was the first time I heard Willie," said Darryl.

Darryl met Willie in 1994 when Darryl programmed for WCKY in Cincinnati. WCKY is now WKRC and, like WLW, is owned by Clear Channel.

"We have a clear direction on where we're going with the radio station and the target audience of the radio station. It's the 41-year-old guy. Topics are normally discussed with producer Rich Walburg. Willie and I will hook up on the phone normally, during the week a few times, as well. Rich is the point person. But we focus on a 41-year-old guy. This means we hit money issues, men's health issues, and whatever a 41-year-old male audience is talking about," Darryl explained.

"I was the quote of the week in the *Cincinnati Enquirer* once. They were criticizing us for some double entendre topic. My comment was something about the fact that if we had a stripper on every six weeks it would not get us big ratings," laughs Darryl.

Willie gets himself in trouble every once in awhile and Darryl is the guy who has to get him out. Often it's a comment off base or a topic taken too far. "Many times what it ends up being is a topic that an advertiser doesn't particularly care for, and you know it's all about ratings and revenue. Rule Number One: Ratings and Revenue. The advertisers, depending on how much they spend on the radio station, obviously get more clout," Darryl said.

"I remember one instance involving the American car dealers. I was involved in it. Willie said he ran the ball down to the goal line and I took it over the line. It's all about discourse. It's all about conversation. It's all about ratings and revenue. It's all about being able to cut through the noise. Willie certainly does that when it comes to radio. There will always be difficult things discussed on the radio station. Whether it comes from a local sports figure like a Reds baseball player, a Bengals player, both teams we have a partnership with, or whether it comes with advertisers we have a partnership with. There will be times we are going to cross the line and the person on the receiving end is going to think it's unfair or uncalled for to be talked about. But at the end of the day, we are aware of where the line is as far as offending sensibilities. You'll never hear Willie attack somebody personally," explains Darryl.

From being a very small part of the radio station as a guest host, show guest and also as a listener, Willie and WLW do a very good job of calling it the way they see it without crossing the line with respect to the Bengals and the Reds. Clear Channel and 700WLW in 2008 sent out a memorandum that at the top of the hour, before the newsbreak: their talk show hosts were to say — "Home of the Best Bengals Coverage." First, Willie mocked the 2008 Bengals with — "More coverage than they deserve." He then shifted to — "Home of the Washington Generals." The Generals of course were the team that always lost to the Harlem Globetrotters. The problem is the Bengals and Reds have been very bad now for a very long time. This is especially true of the Bengals.

Paul Brown was the founder and head coach of the Cleveland

Browns from 1946 to 1962. The Browns won seven championships in the AFL. Despite this success, on January 9, 1963, Art Modell fired Paul Brown. In 1967, Paul Brown secured a franchise for Cincinnati and the AFL.

Paul Brown was an innovator in the game. From training, to passing, to planning, to equipment, Paul Brown was a football legend. From 1937 to 1942, a Cincinnati Bengals team played in the AFL, so Paul Brown used the Bengals name.

The Bengals would play in a new facility named Riverfront Stadium. They shared the facility with the Cincinnati Reds. In 1970, with the AFL/NFL merger complete, both the Browns and Bengals were placed in the AFC Central. A great rivalry was born.

Before they played at Riverfront, the Bengals played at Nippert Stadium on the University of Cincinnati campus. The team finished 3-11 their first year. Paul Brown would coach the team the first eight years.

In 1975, the Bengals went 11-3, but lost to the Oakland Raiders 31-28 in the wild card game. The Bengals made it to the Super Bowl in 1981 and 1989. They lost to the 49ers both times.

Paul Brown died in 1990, and Mike Brown, his son, took over the team. For one stint, under Mike Brown, the team posted 14 consecutive losing seasons. These included years where Don Shula's son, David Shula, coached the team. He now works for his father's Steak House business. David attended Dartmouth College. He played one year in 1981 as a wide receiver and kickoff returner for the Baltimore Colts. He joined his father's coaching staff at Miami in 1982. He became the offensive coordinator with Dallas from 1989-1990. Dallas would demote him. He became an assistant with Cincinnati in 1991.

In 1992, Shula became head coach of the Bengals at age 32. In four and a half years, the Bengals compiled a 19-53 record.

In 2000, Paul Brown Stadium was built on the backs of taxpayers. Mike Brown had threatened to move the franchise to another city. The Bengals hired Marvin Lewis in 2003 and their prospects improved for a while. However, by 2008, the Bengals were again one of the worst teams in the NFL.

The Cincinnati Reds, formerly the Red Stockings, were the first professional baseball team. Founded as an amateur club in 1963, in 1969, it became professional. From 1869 to 1870, the Reds won 130 straight games.

Little known to history, many players from the Cincinnati Red Stockings became in 1870 the Boston Red Stockings. In 1889, the Cincinnati team dropped the "Stockings" from their name.

In 1912, Crosley Field opened and would be the home of the Reds until 1970. The Reds won the National League Pennant in 1919. They would defeat the Chicago White Sox in the World Series in eight games, which was part of the "Black Sox" scandal involving eight players on the White Sox allegedly throwing the World Series. The movie *Eight Men Out* dramatized the story.

In 1931, with the Great Depression, the Reds went bankrupt.

The Crosley brothers, Powel and Lewis, bought the Reds out of bankruptcy in 1933. Powell Crosley founded Crosley Broadcasting Company and WLW radio. In 1935, Crosley Field hosted the first major league night game. In 1938, Johnny Vander Meer threw back-to-back no-hitters, a feat unmatched in baseball.

In 1939, the Reds won the National League but were swept by the New York Yankees in the World Series. In 1940, they defeated the Detroit Tigers in the World Series.

In 1944, Joe Nuxhall would pitch in a game at the age of only 15. In 1954, Ted Kluszewski was the NL home run leader. In 1956, Frank Robinson won the Rookie of the Year. In 1961, the Reds won the NL but lost again to the Yankees. In 1966, the Reds traded Frank Robinson to the Baltimore Orioles. He would win the Triple Crown, the MVP in the American League and lead Baltimore to its first World Series title.

Then came the Big Red Machine. In 1967, Bob Howsam became the General Manager. Dodging a move to San Diego, the City and the County built Riverfront Stadium. In 1970, the first year at Riverfront, the Reds won the National League Pennant only to lose to Baltimore in the World Series. Also in 1970, the Reds hired George "Sparky" Anderson as the manager. The Reds also would win the 1973 NL Pennant, but lose to the Oakland A's.

Through their farm system and a few trades, the Reds would put on the field what many consider the best eight to take the field as a group. Their batting order and position were as follows:

Pete Rose, Third Base

Ken Griffey, Right Field

Joe Morgan, Second Base

George Foster, Left Field

Johnny Bench, Catcher

Tony Perez, First Base

Dave Concepcion, Shortstop

Cesar Geronimo, Center

They would win the 1975 World Series over the Boston Red Sox. In 1976, they would sweep the New York Yankees.

Pete Rose, Johnny Bench, and Joe Morgan are members of the all-century team. Pete Rose is the all-time hits leader. He is a Hall of Famer, not in the Hall of Fame.

Bench and Morgan are considered the best to ever play their positions. Both are in the Hall of Fame.

Tony Perez is in the Hall of Fame. Davey Concepcion is the best shortstop not in the Hall of Fame and belongs in Coopertown.

Griffey had speed and defense, and he could hit for average. Foster won RBI and home run titles. Geronimo was a Gold Glover, as were Bench, Morgan and Concepcion.

In 1990, the Reds under manager Lou Piniella would lead "wire-to-wire" and sweep the Oakland A's in the World Series.

Since that time, it's been painful to be a Reds fan.

It's a touchy area. I'm confident there are times when the Reds and/or Bengals players and coaches get upset. But Willie and WLW would lose credibility if they were completely muzzled. And, besides, the last fifteen-plus years have been terrible for the Reds and Bengals.

"I gotta tell you, when the push back comes is when they're having bad seasons," Darryl said. "If they're having a good season, and every seat in the stadium is filled, and they can't stop selling the hot dogs and the baseball caps, everything is great. Losing seasons brings tenderness!"

Besides being the program director, Darryl is a great talk show host. He fills in, and does a Saturday morning show. On the Big One, Darryl, as host, is promoted for his Saturday morning show as "Dangerous" Darryl Parks. And "dangerous" he is in the minds of many of the regular callers.

"Willie is probably the best talk show host I've ever been associated with," Darryl said. "I think if you look on the national level, he's got to be in the top one or two percent of talk show hosts. Many times criticism comes because of the difficult message or topic or the fulcrum angle the topic has taken on when Willie takes on a topic on the air. But Willie gets it."

"At the end of the day, Willie's an entertainer. I just had a conversation with somebody recently and they were talking about their agenda and how people want to hear what they want to talk about. I said it has nothing to do with your agenda. It has to do with what people are talking about. I think one of the great things that Willie does is he owns a story. If something happens in Cincinnati, he attaches his name to it. He is very, very good at that. I have used the example with other people here in the building. The dude is like a pig to a trough. He grabs a story and attaches his name to it. He is keenly aware of making himself a news-maker in the market."

"When we partnered with Channel 5, the local NBC television station, one of the first things their news director said to me was that Willie's breaking stories a week and a half or two weeks before they hit the news."

"I had worked with him for years and I knew he was doing that, but I had never really thought about it until that was said to me. And it's very true; with his connections, he breaks stories," Darryl explained.

There's a partnership with WLW and WLWT.

"The beautiful thing about our relationship is the relationship is based upon business needs. With Channel 5 there's a heritage that goes back there. But who the hell remembers 1963? There are common call letters. But the business needs are based in making Channel 5's on-air people personalities. We certainly utilize their personalities, whether it is their main anchors, chief meteorologists or Brian Hamrick who is on with Willie a bit. There's that cross-promotion. Channel 5 certainly uses us too. Willie is a great example. Willie has been on set as their legal expert during the Marcus Fiesel trials and obviously during the elections. So there's a great relationship there with Channel 5. It's just based upon common business needs. The great thing about it, as opposed to our former partner, Channel 5 gets it. They get that Willie, or any of the other personalities on the station, may make fun of them or may call them out when they predict 14 inches of snow and it rains," Darryl said. "Willie refers to the weather team as the 'weather terrorists' when they scare the hell out of everyone with their false prediction of 'white death.'"

They even accept the sexual innuendo. Willie gets away with sexual innuendo like no other. Channel 5 News anchors Sandra Ali and Sheree Paolello brought him a blueberry pie and some cookies live on the air. I was lucky I was in the studio that day, and it was my funniest day of being in the station, when they brought their pie and cookies.

"We all want to be considered serious, but there's a reason there are two very good looking women anchors," laughs Darryl Parks.

"Willie can be using humor and then shift gears in a minute and give a somber sobriety take on a story like firemen being killed. He provides the appropriate solemnity to a story. He'll make the appropriate humor and satire, because Americans love satire. There's a rule of thumb in talk radio that you have to affect people in two ways, monetarily or emotionally. And he is keenly aware of affecting people emotionally. He did an interview last week with a young boy, Parker Hunt. The boy had to have a heart transplant. Frankly, ninety-nine percent of the other talk show hosts in this country would have done that interview, and it would have been boring. He brought out emotion," explains Darryl.

After Rule Number One — ratings and revenue — Darryl points out Rule Number Two: "Rule number two is never let the truth get in the way of a good talk show." Willie follows Rule Number One and Two. Darryl explains that if playing polka music

24/7 increased ratings and revenue, 700WLW would play polka music.

"Rich Walburg lines up guests for Willie. Guests give a mental outline. Willie does not use notes. He does not have an outline of what he's going to talk about. Willie simply lives his life to prepare. He's always prepping. I'll give you the example. I had an opportunity to travel with him a couple years ago to Washington, D.C. We spent the weekend together in Washington. He was constantly on his phone. He's constantly working. His daily life is his show prep. He triples Rush Limbaugh in the local market. That's unique. There's not a lot of radio stations that would put such a good talent out against Rush. But Willie's talent is so great that it's not any competition," explains Darryl.

In 2008, the Bengals had a disastrous year with a record of 2-15-1.

Willie referred to Marvin Lewis as Marvin Shula.

Marvin Lewis began coaching as a graduate assistant for Idaho State, then was their linebacker coach from 1981-1984. He coached at Long Beach State in 1985, the University of Mexico 1987-1989 and University of Pittsburgh from 1990-1992. He moved up to the big time with internships at Kansas City Chiefs and San Francisco 49ers. He became the linebackers coach for the Pittsburgh Steelers for four seasons from 1992-1996. In 1996, he became defensive coordinator for the Baltimore Ravens. He held that position until 2001. The Ravens won Super Bowl XXXV behind a great defense. They allowed the fewest rushing yards (970) and fewest paints (165) in a 16 game season. In 2002, he became the defensive coordinator and assistant head coach for the 2002 season.

On January 14, 2003, he became the Bengals' ninth head coach. He actually beat out Tom Loughlin for the job. From 2003-2007, his second was 42-38 regular season record. The Bengals finished 8-8 his first two seasons. In 2005, they were 11-5, won the AFC North, but lost to the Steelers 31-17 in the wild card round.

However, by 2008, the Bengals had imploded and Marvin Lewis had been what Willie called "Bengalized." This is a word for incompetence and futility.

CHAPTER 25

NIGHT TO DAY

"Go as far as you can see; when you get there,
you'll be able to see farther."

J.P. Morgan

Willie won't reveal what he earns for his three hour a day job. In 1990, published reports were he made $50,000 for his nine to midnight slot. Considering he gave up his law practice for the daytime slot, he obviously makes a significant salary. I'm confident he probably pulls down more than anyone in radio in Cincinnati.

In 1999, Willie held the job as program director of 700WLW. Mike McConnell was hosting nine a.m. to two p.m., and Gary Burbank was hosting two to six and both wanted to work fewer hours. McConnell is today's WLW's 9 a.m. to noon man. "Midday" is his show. Premiere Radio Networks picked it up for national syndication in July 2006. He also does the *Weekend with Mike McConnell* on Saturdays. Gary Burbank was a popular WLW radio personality. He worked at the station from 1981 to his sign-off on December 21, 2007. His real name is Billy Purser. Burbank developed different characters and developed a unique voice for each.

Earl Pitts, American, [a character] was a full-blooded redneck who made daily commentary on everything from politics to family to friends. He began every segment with: "Do you know what makes me sick." He ended the spot with: "This is Earl Pitts,

Umerikan, Pitts off!" Burbank's Earl Pitts daily "commentaries" are syndicated throughout the country on about 200 stations.

Gilbert Gnarley, a senior citizen, [character] made crank calls to various businesses and people. Remarkably, those who answered were played for a pretty long time. Gilbert would ask an obvious stupid question and keep asking them.

The Right Rev. Deuteronomy Skaggs, [character] was a radio preacher who encouraged listeners to "dig in them jeans and pull out them greens" (money). Burbank's cast of characters was endless.

Burbank regularly satirized former Cincinnati mayor Jerry Springer, along with other local politicians, newscasters, and celebrities, such as former Cincinnati Reds owner "Saint CEO" Marge Schott. He satirized and lampooned the struggling. Satirical radio serials were also used to lampoon the (often struggling) Reds baseball team during the postseason playoffs ("The Hunt for the Reds' October") and the Cincinnati Bengals ("All My Bengals"). They played like the soap operas.

Burbank has won several major awards, including back-to-back Marconi Awards as Large Market Personality of the Year in 1990 and 1991. Willie has won the Marconi too, in 2001.

Willie, as program director, recommended to the powers to be that Willie be on from twelve to three. This move allowed Mike McConnell to go nine to noon, and allowed Gary Burbank to do three to six. It took Willie off nights, which has only about twenty percent of the daytime listeners.

Randy Michaels rejected Willie's plan. He called it a "stupid idea." Randy believed Willie's style would never work during the day. At night, Willie could do his act. Willie claimed he would change his act. He knew what not to do during the day. The indecent harbor is after 10 p.m. He knew that. He'd change it. Michaels still said no. Willie sent a memo to Michaels stating he would do it, and if Michaels didn't like it he could find somebody else to do the job as program director.

Willie received a call from one of his subordinates informing him that Randy Michaels was, in fact, going to find somebody else to be the program director. The "new guy" was Darryl Parks.

Originally from Buffalo, Parks worked in Columbus, Ohio, at the time. Darryl listened to 700WLW from Columbus and determined there should be a twelve to three. He agreed with Willie.

"I've been trying to do that," I told Darryl, "but I can't get it done," explained Willie.

"I'll tell Randy it is simply time and I'll come up with something, and we'll just do it. You will have one rating book to have better ratings. If it works, I can convince Randy. But, you have to have better ratings. Otherwise, I've got nothing to work with," Darryl replied.

Willie did it. Ratings doubled. Randy Michaels agreed it was a great idea.

"Willie sounds great," Randy said to Darryl. The rest is history. It's worked for nine years.

"I had to quit my law practice, because when I was working at night I had all day to do other things. But when you work twelve to three and you've got to get down to the station about eleven, it's in the middle of the day. So I had to quit my law practice. I still handle a few cases because I like going to court now and then," Willie says. He is still licensed to practice law in Ohio.

Willie never liked being program director. He found himself at odds with the other radio personalities. He found himself on the opposite side of the hosts.

He had to tell Gary Burbank when a "skit" was not funny. He had to tell Mike McConnell he had to be more topical. He had to tell Jim Scott to pick up the pace in the morning. He had to tell Cris Collinsworth to stay on topic.

Cris Collinsworth was the *Sports Talk* host who followed Bob Trumpy in the slot. Bob Trumpy played tight end for the Cincinnati Bengals from 1968-1977. He is now is a radio analyst for CBS Radio Sports/Westwood One.

After football, the opinionated Trumpy hosted *Sports Talk* in the evenings on 700WLW from 1980-1989. He left for television assignments for NBC Sports, including the Olympics.

In late 2008, Trumpy began reappearing one night a week as a guest on *Sports Talk*. He still lives in Cincinnati. Cris Collinsworth left *Sports Talk* in 1998, and Andy Furman took over. Collinsworth is now a national television sports figure. He's also one of the classiest members of the media and one heck of an athlete. In 1976, he won the Florida Class 3A 100-yard dash state championship. "Not bad for a white guy," said Willie. At the University of Florida, Collinsworth became an All-American wide receiver. The Cincinnati Bengals picked him in the second round of the 1981 NFL Draft.

At 6'5" and possessing speed, he became a reliable NFL receiver. He made the Pro Bowl in 1981, 1982 and 1983. He played in Super Bowl XVI and XXIII with the Bengals.

No "dumb athlete," Collinsworth earned a law degree from the University of Cincinnati College of Law. He married Holly Bankamper, a law school classmate, and he, his wife and their children live in the Cincinnati area in Fort Thomas, Kentucky.

Collinsworth, after his football career, became a guest host for Bob Trumpy on 700WLW before taking over for Trumpy, who moved on to television.

Next, Collinsworth became a reporter for HBO's *Inside the NFL*. In 1990, he joined NBC's team and did color for NFL and college games. He joined the NBC *NFL Pregame Show* in 1996. In 1998, he joined FOX. In 2006, he was co-hosting *Inside the NFL*, serving as NBC studio analyst for Sunday night and color commentary for the NFL network. In 2009, Collinsworth filled John Madden's color position on *Sunday Night Football* alongside Al Michaels — two great broadcasters with a Cincinnati history.

Collinsworth has won Emmys for his work. It all began on the Big One 700WLW.

"It's hard to tell your co-patriots they're doing something wrong. I found that hard to do because they would say, who the hell are you? Well, I'm the program director. Damn. I had to keep Collinsworth in line and now he's big time," laughs Willie.

In sum, there is no more talented assemblage of radio talent than 700WLW. Jim Scott, the morning man, won a Marconi as the best in the nation the same as Willie. Mike McConnell, from 9 a.m. to noon, is the voice of common sense and was nominated for a Marconi. When Gary Burbank handled afternoons, 700WLW had talent that had been awarded five Marconi's as well as other awards.

CHAPTER 26

WWF AND WILLIE

"Sliding head first is the safest way to get to the next base, I think, and the fastest. You don't lose your momentum, and there's one more important reason I slide head first, it gets my picture in the paper."

Pete Rose

*T*he entertainment world found a perfect collaboration when the World Wrestling Federation and Willie hooked up. When the WWF would come to Cincinnati, on occasion Willie received an invitation to emcee matches. Willie became a regular. He received the opportunity to meet the entire cast of characters: Hulk Hogan, Macho Man Randy Savage and Rowdy Roddy Piper.

One late night in the 1990s, while hanging out at the Drawbridge Inn in Fort Mitchell, Kentucky, just south of Cincinnati, Rowdy Roddy Piper had one too many to drink. This resulted in his being picked up for a DUI. He called on Willie to defend him and Willie accepted.

Behind the scenes, Willie, as most defense attorneys do, worked out a deal with the prosecutor for Rowdy. In a first offense DUI in Kentucky, a defendant can dodge jail time. A license suspension, fine and court costs is the deal you want. Of course, there is the pain of insurance rates going up. However, escaping jail is the key and Willie had that handled.

On the day scheduled for Willie and Rowdy to attend Kenton

District Court and make the plea of guilty and take the deal, Rowdy flew in to Greater Cincinnati Airport. Willie drove out himself and picked Rowdy up.

As Rowdy walked off the airplane, Willie could not help but be taken by Rowdy's dress. He had upon his head a blue University of Kentucky baseball cap, and he wore a satin blue University of Kentucky sweat suit. Rowdy was the walking embodiment of a true blue University of Kentucky fan.

"Damn Rowdy. Don't you think you overdid it a little bit?" Willie asked.

"Hey. This is Kentucky. I'm not taking any chances. You have to be prepared to do anything you can to influence the judge favorably," Rowdy said.

"O.K., I guess," replied Willie.

They hung out a little while, ate lunch, and then drove to the Courthouse for the awaited time of 1:00 p.m.

The case against Rowdy Roddy Piper, although only a misdemeanor, caused high level of local media coverage. It led the local news on television and appeared in daily newspapers due to the legendary pro wrestler's representation by a noted lawyer/radio personality. The date, time, and location of the hearing was well publicized.

As Rowdy and Willie entered the Kenton County Courthouse, everyone immediately recognized Willie and this mammoth of a man in a satin blue sweat suit walking next to him. People came up to shake Rowdy's hand, get an autograph and even have a photograph taken for the one or two that happened to have a camera. Several shouted — "Piper's Pit! Piper's Pit!"

Willie and Rowdy made it to the courtroom and took seats near the front where lawyers always do to wait for the call of their case. Willie checked in with the prosecutor to insure all was still good, and it was.

The Judge came into the courtroom and court was called to order. The prosecutor called Rowdy's case and Willie and Rowdy walked to the podium. Rowdy gave his name, date of birth and address for identification purposes. The prosecutor made the recommendation. The Court asked Rowdy if he was prepared to plead guilty. Rowdy stated yes.

Then, Willie thought a curve ball was coming. "Mr. Piper, there's one problem," said the Judge.

"What's that?" responded Willie on behalf of his client. Willie got a sick feeling in his stomach.

"I'm a University of Louisville graduate and Cardinal fan," said the Judge.

Without hesitation and not missing a beat, Rowdy ripped open the front of his sweat suit to reveal a bright red Louisville Cardinal #1 t-shirt to the Judge. He then spun around and showed it to the entire crowd gathered in Court. The place unleashed laughter usually restricted in Court.

So impressed with this response, the Court waived the fine, assessed only costs, and hit the gavel to conclude the matter.

Willie and Rowdy walked out of the courtroom. As they did, Rowdy leaned over to Willie "I was prepared for everything," whispered Rowdy.

Never underestimate the entertainment talent of the WWF.

CHAPTER 27

RATINGS AND REVENUE AND THE VOICE OF THE COMMON MAN

"Good leadership consists of showing average people how to do the work of superior people."

John D. Rockefeller

I n many aspects, radio is the same as any business, and in other ways, it's unique. What is important is not unique. "Ratings and revenues. That's all that matters," says Willie, echoing the Darryl Parks mantra. As mentioned before, Darryl Parks claims if 700WLW would receive the highest ratings and revenues playing polka music, polka music would fill the airwaves.

Willie has always been irreverent. Satire, sexual innuendo, and bravado are all a part of Willie's game. This supplemented his serious interviews and political analyses.

The Fun Ladies were regulars on Willie's show. They sold sex toys. Willie told them if they needed any research and development to let him know.

Dave Reinhart was a former program director at WLW. One of Willie's favorite stories is the night he called the Newport Police on Reinhard. Willie told the story to *Cincinnati* magazine during an interview for the magazine.

"I had a stripper on the show one night for my birthday. She worked at the Brass Ass. Reinhart took her back to Newport. He was going to come back to the show and an hour and a half later, I said on the air, 'Where in the hell is Reinhart?' So I called the Newport Police and said, 'Our program director Dave Reinhart is on stage at the Brass Ass, he's got his fly open, a WEBN t-shirt on, a propeller beanie, and he's doing the strip. Hurry up and go get him.' I told them I was Bill Cunningham at WLW; I thought they knew it was a joke. I then called back ten minutes later and said he had been seen in a Kroger shopping cart with a twelve-foot high orange flag, rolling down Monmouth Street. The dispatcher was acting as if he knew who I was. But they were sending Newport police cars all over the downtown area, trying to find Reinhart. They didn't know it was a joke."

"The next day, the shit hit the fan," Willie said. They were over at the studio and they were going to file a police report against me for a false police report. I had to go to Newport City Council that next Wednesday and apologize to the city. Channel 12 News came over and filmed it. There were two cops there; the mayor had the complaint in his hand, and my lawyer was telling me if I cracked a smile or made fun of them in any way, they were going to arrest me on the spot. So I had this shit-eatin' grin on my face, and I had to go to the men's room to laugh and get it out of my system."

"You get ratings by having large numbers of people listen to you. And you get people listening to you by being entertaining. You can read books and magazines to get information. You can watch television and see a collision, fire, or crime. But talk radio is theater of the mind. It has to be about entertainment. People love to laugh and to be entertained. They enjoy a radio talk show host saying things which they don't have the ability to say or saying things they don't hear expressed in other parts of the media," according to Willie.

"A good radio talk show host makes the listeners laugh and makes them listen because so many American's viewpoints are not expressed by newspapers or television. So, the role of a talk show host, number one, is get ratings and revenues. And we get revenues and ratings by connecting emotionally with the listeners who want to get in their car and listen to us as they drive somewhere. I've had hundreds of people tell me that they schedule their lunch based upon my radio talk show," Willie boasts.

"Too many talk show hosts think they're talking to 100,000 people in one place and refer to "you people." In reality, in radio, you are talking to one person one-on-one. So when I do a talk show I think of a 41-year-old male who is married with two kids. I think about what are the problems in his life today. I think of a person that I talk to. I often talk to my producer, because I want him to be the substitute for the listener. In talk radio, you do not talk to 100,000 people. You talk to one person. I often say, it is you and me. I want the listeners to hear me talking to them inside their heads, and they are listening to me, that one person. Too many in talk radio use the plural. I always try to use the singular," explains Willie.

In the early 1990s, Willie proclaimed himself the "Voice of the Common Man." National television personality Jerry Springer, former Mayor of Cincinnati and WLWT Channel 5 News Anchor, would close his show with "take care of yourself and each other." As an example, Willie scoffs at Springer's adieu. "That sounded a bit too socialist for me," laughs Willie. In 1971, Jerry Springer was elected to Cincinnati City Council. In 1974, he resigned after writing a check to a prostitute. The police in Fort Wright, Kentucky, across the river from Cincinnati during a raid of a "massage parlor" found a check Jerry Springer wrote. He fell on his sword and admitted the ordeal. The public forgave him and he won back the council seat in 1975. In 1977, he was elected mayor of the City. In 1982, Springer ran for the Democratic nomination for Ohio Governor. He lost. However, in 1991, *The Jerry Springer Show* debuted from Chicago and was a hit. While he was still in Cincinnati, Clear Channel's rock station WEBN, allowed Springer to give commentaries under *The Springer Memorandum*. He gained a job as a political commentator on NBC affiliate WLWT. He became the news anchor. He ended each show with, "Take care of yourself, and each other." He would win ten local Emmy Awards and would be the most popular news anchor in Cincinnati.

"I came up with the Voice of the Common Man. I decided to play off the idea that I am not an elitist. I am not a country club Republican. I am a Wal-Mart Republican. So I made it up, the voice of the common man and woman," explains Willie.

Next, Willie granted himself and others who he believes in the title — Great American.

"I came up with that in around 1992 or so. I have great respect for talk radio listeners. Unlike those who read newspapers, or those who watch television, talk radio listeners are the backbone of the nation. Most are married. Most never get divorced. Most own cars. Most own homes. Most have kids. Most have the same problems I have. If you listen to talk radio, you're more likely to be educated and have more assets, be more successful, and have more of a supple intellect than other audiences that watch or listen or read other medias. The talk radio audience is special, unique, and different. So when I say 'You are a great American,' I'm referring to the listeners of talk radio who work to make this country work more than welfare chiselers, work more than social degenerates, and work more than the angle shooters that are out there all the time. But when I meet talk radio listeners, when I meet my P-1s, as they're called in the industry, it's a tight circle. They're almost always people just like me," explains Willie. Willie believes a Great American is someone who plays by the rules and defends the American way of life. You do not need to be famous, just make America better. John Wayne, John Glenn, and Ronald Reagan are three famous Great Americans on Willie's list. Willie actually not only has, but also admits to having a life size cardboard cutout of John Wayne and Rick Pitino in his bedroom. Willie worries too many Americans pursue almighty dollar more than higher values. At the top of Willie's list of Great Americans is the American soldier who had freed most of the world from Nazis, Communists, dictators, and butchers like Saddam Hussein.

Days after the 2008 Presidential election, a caller called into Michael Savage's nightly national radio show and began his comments with, "You're a great American." Savage went bonkers. He began a tirade against the caller. He told the caller to never call him a Great American because he was just an American like everyone else. He yelled, "That is a phrase from a 'tin horn lawyer' who sounds like Groucho Marx." Without using Willie's name, Savage ripped Willie.

Willie's response was to use Savage's tirade as part of his show. Savage ironically is on Clear Channel's 55 WKRC, 700WLW's sister station.

Next, Willie added to his mantle of titles — "The Conscience of the American People."

"I like to think a conscience is something more than a thought. A conscience has a moral overtone. Most Americans who listen to talk radio have a moral side. If you're listening to talk radio, you're more likely to go to church than those who don't listen to talk radio," Willie explains.

"I always said that voters are people who read the newspapers, watch the news, or go to church. Those are your voters. And they listen to talk radio. Talk radio is interactive. If you read something you don't like, you may send a letter to the editor, and it may not get published. If you watch Brian Williams on NBC news do a story you disagree with, you can't respond. But in talk radio, some schlep in Schenectady can pick up the phone and suddenly he's equal with me. He's in the media himself. He's interactive. He's connected. This is why talk radio works in the 21st Century. The 21st Century is about inter-connective connectibilities between various platforms. And talk radio is the only platform where you can connect and be equal to the host. The 'Conscience of the American People' means there's a moral tone and moral overlay relative to some person's life. I like to think I have a conscience and I like to think I live my life that way. Because if I would do something wrong, it would get in the newspapers. If I would drive drunk, or if I would do something wrong with a child, I would not only lose my job, I would be prosecuted, and it would embarrass 200,000 people who listen to me every day, and maybe a million on my syndicated show. It would be embarrassing. I would be a hypocrite. It would affect them if I did that.

And so I have a viewpoint that I have to be careful what I say and what I do, because it would impact not just my family, but it would hurt people who rely upon me," states Willie in a rare serious tone.

Penny has always supported Willie's radio career.

"I was shocked when he told me the first time he was going to have his own radio show. Prior to that news, he and Leslie Gaines had appeared on Alan Browning's show," Penny recalls.

"I never gave it a thought he'd become a radio talk show host. I do remember on the first few nights, he would call me and tell me to call in because he was worried he wouldn't have any callers. So I'd call in," laughs Penny.

Penny doesn't tune into Willie's shows now.

"You have to understand, when he first began he was on nine to midnight," Penny said. "Well, I was in law school when he started. He would leave the house around eight o'clock or sometimes a little bit before. We had Evan, and I would be helping Evan with schoolwork and so on and so forth. Well, I did not begin my own work for law school until maybe nine or nine-thirty. There was no way I was going to be listening to Billy. I had my work cut out for me with law school. I had long days. In evenings, I just did not listen. And sometimes if I did catch him now and then, there would be few things that would happen and I'd be like, no, it's better if I just don't listen."

"But he went to days and then I was working during the day and I couldn't hear him," explains Penny.

Penny says she doesn't ever offer Willie any advice for his radio shows.

The Cunninghams have always maintained the typical American home life.

"Evan was the central focus for us," Penny explains. "We attended movies, relaxed at home, and enjoyed our son's company."

"Now it's the grandchildren, Cole and Avery. We enjoy the typical dinner and movie. I actually have golfed with Billy. He's laid back when I golf with him. A lot of people believe that because he golfs well, that he wouldn't be too patient with me.

I'm tougher on myself. And I don't like the fact that I don't do so well, so I stay away from the course," said Penny. Willie truly connects to the common man and gives that common man a voice and a pulpit.

Golf does not build character. It reveals it. No sport has such highs and lows since the competition is against oneself. Willie has won many local golf tourneys and once finished 14th in the Ohio Amateur. He carries a one handicap.

CHAPTER 28

CLINTON AND GORE

The Clinton eight years in the White House were heaven for Willie.

"Those were the heydays along with Monica Lewinsky. That was the best," Willie said. "That went on for months about the fun because that story involved politics, sex, power, hot chicks, oral sex, cigars-everything. Everything a man enjoys. So I thought it was a great topic for talk radio."

Then in 2008, Willie had Hillary Clinton running for president. A native of Illinois, Hillary Rodham first attracted national attention in 1969 for her remarks as the first student to deliver the commencement address at Wellesley College. She embarked on a career in law after graduating from Yale Law School in 1973. Following a stint as a Congressional legal counsel, she moved to Arkansas in 1974, and married Bill Clinton in 1975. She was later named the first female partner at Rose Law Firm in 1979, and was twice listed as one of the one hundred most influential lawyers in America. She was the First Lady of Arkansas from 1979 to 1981 and 1983 to 1992 and was active in a number of organizations concerned with child welfare, as well as sitting on the boards of Wal-Mart and several other corporations.

First Lady of the United States Hillary Clinton's major initiative (the Clinton health care plan) failed to gain approval from the U.S. Congress in 1994. In 1997 and 1999, Clinton played a role in advocating for the establishment of the State Children's Health Insurance Program, the Adoption and Safe Families Act, and the

Foster Care Independence Act. She became the only First Lady to be subpoenaed, testifying before a federal grand jury because of the Whitewater controversy in 1996. She was never charged with any wrongdoing in this or any of the several other investigations during her husband's administration. The state of her marriage to Bill Clinton was the subject of considerable public discussion following the Lewinsky scandal in 1998.

After moving to New York, Clinton was elected as senator for New York State in 2000. That election marked the first time an American First Lady had run for public office; Clinton is also the first female senator to represent New York. In the Senate, she initially supported the George W. Bush administration on some foreign policy issues, which included voting for Iraq War Resolution. She has subsequently opposed the administration on its conduct of the Iraq War, and has opposed it on most domestic issues. She was re-elected by a wide margin in 2006. In the 2008 presidential nomination race, Clinton succeeded in winning more primaries and delegates than any other woman in U.S. history.

Willie actually encouraged Ohio voters to vote for Hillary in the 2008 primaries to prolong the Democratic primary battle. Always the troublemaker, he joined in Rush Limbaugh's idea of having Republicans vote Democratic for Hillary in the Ohio primary. Hillary would win the Ohio primary. Willie was successful since Hillary won the Ohio Democrat Primary over Barack Hussein Obama.

The Gore/Bush election in 2000 provided more great radio. Willie described things well: "It went on from the election until my birthday, which was December 11. Every day for five weeks. I was on the air six days a week. And I kept waiting for Bush to get screwed because I knew that the Democrats had better lawyers and I knew the Florida Supreme Court would rule. And I had real doubt whether the U.S. Supreme Court would ever take the case. Shockingly they did and by a five to four vote — but it was seven to two on the issue of equal protection."

CHAPTER 29

WILLIE'S POLITICAL PHILOSOPHY

"Be not simply good; be good for something."

Thoreau

Considering Willie is a radio talk show host, I'll not cheat him out of his espousing his political philosophy in his own words. I asked him what his political philosophy was in an interview and his answer, which he delivered off the top of his head, follows:

"I'm more libertarian than conservative. I've developed a belief that government is too large, too distant and too corrupt. The present American political system is inherently crippled. The only possibility we have of remaining a great nation is to free ourselves from the shackles of bureaucracy, regulation, taxes, and government oversight. I inherently distrust government and bureaucrats. I think the role of government is to eliminate from our path the obstacles that would allow us to succeed. The role of government is not to establish a department of happiness. The role of government is to allow us to pursue happiness on our own, as we define happiness, whether we're butchers, bakers, or candlestick makers, teachers, nurses, truck drivers.

"I like people having their individual lives as unaltered as possible by the tentacles of government. I don't think there should be a lot of drug laws. I don't think taxes should be very high at all. I think government rules and regulations should be inherently cut. I'm always nauseated when government is meeting in legislatures, general assemblies, city hall, or in the Congress, because their role is to inflict themselves upon us. Their role is not to free us, to make us all that we can be. The Constitution guarantees to each of us the pursuit of happiness. It does not guarantee us happiness. It's up to us to seek it and to pursue it. Too many consider there's a department of happiness in government to which we should go and apply, instead of a government eliminating from our path the obstacles to our pursuit.

"When I think of the Democrat Party today, it is pro-abortion, which means they think abortion is a sacrament. It is anti-military. It is anti-God. It is in favor of illegal alien migration into America. It opposes tax cuts. It wants more government spending. In other words, it is directly opposite of what the Founding Fathers intended, and directly opposite of what I believe. In the 2008 primary election of Ohio, I could have signed a statement in which I switched parties to vote in the primary. But I had to sign a statement that says I believe in the principles of the Democratic Party. And the way it is constituted today, I could not, in good conscience, sign that statement. When John F. Kennedy was president, I could have signed it. John F. Kennedy gave us tax cuts and pay any price, carry any burden, defend any friend, oppose any foe. That's not the modern Democrat Party, which began, I guess, with George McGovern in 1972, and is best exhibited by the statements of Barack Hussein Obama who campaigned to increase federal spending. I think both parties are inherently corrupt, since their only true role in government is to guarantee their political survival. They don't do the people's business; they do their own.

"The Bush administration and the Republican leadership has been a failure. The spending under this so-called compassionate conservative has not been very compassionate or conservative. We build bridges in Baghdad instead of across Ohio.

"I'm always hesitating to criticize what's happening in Iraq because the policy of this administration is being carried out by the American soldier, who is the most stainless character in world history.

"Whenever some man or woman, generally of tender years, decides to step forward and say, send me, and they put their life and limb at risk, and they put on the uniform of my country, and they go and defend us against the savages in Iraq and Afghanistan, I am hard pressed to criticize what they do. So even though the Bush policy, after the fall of Baghdad, has been an unmitigated disaster until the surge, it is being carried out by brave American soldiers and other government employees who have done things that I would not want to do. I wish my son not have to do things like put on the colors of this nation for about $600 a month for eighteen hours a day, seven days a week, fighting savages and almost subhumans over there who think its okay to put bombs on the bodies of women and send them into barracks to kill innocent people.

"So, as long as the American soldier is fighting and dying, I'm hard pressed to unduly criticize the policies of the government that they've sworn allegiance to, and to which they're going to go and sacrifice, maybe their lives. I think the Bush administration and Rumsfeld made serious blunders in Iraq on planning, on execution, on billions of dollars that can't be located, on bribing officials with American dollars, on building schools that are blown up and bridges that don't function in Iraq.

"But, on the other hand, what do you do when 4,000 soldiers have been killed and 25,000 wounded? Because by criticizing the Bush policy, I think by innuendo you're criticizing those who implement the policy.

"The best thing about the Bush administration is that he believes the best defense is a good offense. During the Clinton years, there was a sense that criminal terrorists should be indicted. They should be put on trial. They should be convicted and sentenced. I think they simply should be killed in place where they are. So the Bush administration is going to the caves of Afghanistan and to the killing fields of Somalia and they hunt them down like dogs and bring them to justice. That's the best part of the Bush administration. We don't wait any more and then prosecute after the fact. We keep the terrorists from striking in the first place. If Bill Clinton had done that, thousands more Americans would be alive today.

"But to his defense, in 1993, when the first World Trade Center was bombed, Clinton never went to the World Trade Center in 1993 when it was bombed. The American people didn't ask him to go. No reporter said, "Why didn't you go?" The mindset of the American people was that it was a criminal problem that could be managed. And because of 9/11, Bush took the approach: This isn't a criminal problem, we're at war. And we don't bring Nazis to trial. What we should do is kill them. Bush is correct on that. That's the best part of the Bush administration.

"That's the evil of Obama and Clinton. They take the old-time approach of "let's bring all the troops home. Let's wait to see what happens. Do not eavesdrop with the Patriot Act. Let's not get the cooperation of the telecommunications company and let's wait for them to do something and then we'll indict them." In the meantime, thousands of Americans will die. I don't have any right to lessen a life. So George Bush has kept alive thousands of Americans who otherwise would be dead but for the Patriot Act and other aggressive measures he's taken here and around the globe.

"I think there are three great evils that will destroy this country. Speed limits are not going to destroy the country. Drug use is not going to destroy the country. What could destroy the country is one of three things. Illegal alien migration from the Third World unfettered into America could destroy America because it's changing who we are.

"Second, is the debt crisis? There is about $58 trillion of unfunded promises the federal government has provided to individual Americans: Medicare, Medicaid, and Social Security. The debt crisis could kill us economically. It could trash our currency.

"The third fear is terrorism. Having to live where we can't go to a high school football game without being frisked and searched, or being afraid to go to a mall because our children may be killed, is going to change us. When we are afraid to travel the highways because a .357 bullet may come through the windshield, or we cannot go to public functions without fear of being nuked, it cannot help but change who we are. The three great issues – illegal alien migration, the debt crisis, and terrorism – are things that could destroy America as we know it.

"George Bush is right on only one of those three. He did nothing on the border. He did nothing about the debt crisis. In fact, he has spent like a drunken sailor on shore leave. But he's done something on terrorism. He is one for three. For a major league baseball player, that is good. For a president, it's terrible.

"Two pillars of our society should be government and our banking systems; sadly both are inherently corrupt. The Obama administration spends about one trillion dollars on a worthless stimulus package as Wall Street weasels create complicated investment instruments that spread toxic cancer cells all over the world. If we cannot trust the Roman Catholic Church, bankers, or politicians in Washington, Americans are in deep trouble," argues Willie.

So there you have it: Willie's perspective and his dream and concerns for America as a Great American.

CHAPTER 30

OHIO: STRIPPERS, SMOKERS AND GAMBLERS NEED NOT APPLY

"Keep your face always toward the sunshine
and shadows will fall behind you."

Walt Whitman

illie loves his native state. Like a parent who knows tough love is sometimes the answer, Willie is concerned about his Ohio.

"Ohio politicians, Republicans and Democrats, complain constantly about losing 200,000 jobs. Then they do things to help bring about the loss of more jobs. I don't drink. I don't smoke. I don't go to strip joints, and I don't gamble except on the golf course, which I think is a bet, not a gamble. Ohio has banned smoking in most public places, especially bars and restaurants, which on the border is causing thousands of Ohioans to go to Kentucky, Indiana, Michigan, and West Virginia. That has eliminated thousands of jobs of small business owners at bowling alleys, bars, restaurants, and taverns.

"I had a friend who owns Western Bowl in Cincinnati, Ohio, who told me that for thirty years bowlers would come an hour ahead of time, have a beer or two and a couple cigarettes, sit at the bar, order some food. Then they would bowl for their three games, which would take about an hour to an hour and a half. They would drink beer, have a cigarette or two there. And then

155

after the bowling, they would go to the bar and talk about all the pins that did not get knocked down and have another couple beers and smoke a cigarette or two and then go home.

"Now, they show up five minute before bowling starts, and they leave five minutes after bowling ends because they can't smoke. If they can't smoke, they don't drink, and if they don't drink and smoke, they don't eat. So there are literally thousands and thousands of good paying jobs and thousands of businesses that have been irretrievably damaged by the lawmakers in Columbus who put the issue of smoking on the ballot.

"Two competing issues were in conflict with each other. The voters did not know what they were voting on. But they banned smoking in almost all places unwittingly, which cost thousands of jobs.

"Secondly, strip clubs. It's cost about 10,000 jobs. A special interest group called Citizens for Community Values — and they're not part of the community and they have no values — are a right wing group headed up by a former pornographer named Phil Buress. They got together hundreds of thousands of signatures from the church-goers who thought it was terrible that women, in private, would take off their clothes and show their wares to ogling males. They got hundreds of thousands of those signatures, which demanded that the lawmakers in Columbus pass a law. And if they didn't pass a law, it went on the ballot. So the lawmakers created a hula hoop of three foot separation between the girls and the male customers, which has the effect of eliminating all the fun at a strip club. It is not just the 10,000 jobs that were lost. It is the strippers, the bartenders, the bar backs, the servers, the custodians, the lawyers, the doctors, the property owners — thousands of jobs were blown up by the lawmakers in Columbus because they didn't like the fact that young women wanted to take their clothes off and male customers like to watch. In practically every society, every nation and at anytime in human history, men have enjoyed watching women taking off their clothes — in fact, women also like, at times, getting naked.

"Another thing is gambling. Casino gambling is or will soon

be all around Ohio. Of course the State Lotto is perfect because it's a sucker's bet. The State gambles with pull-tabs. They gamble with the lottery, the Pick 6, the Pick 3, the daily number. We now have this silly game called Keno. What the hell is Keno? And they incentivize, through commercials, Americans to gamble in ridiculous ways, supposedly to support the schools, which never happens. But they don't want flashy casinos in which the gambler's got a fair shot at winning in blackjack, craps, and other games.

"And so now, the right wing, this time, is angry at casinos because they bring in the wrong element, as if the Lotto brings in the right element. Now all around Ohio we've lost tens of thousands of jobs to Indiana, West Virginia, Michigan and soon Kentucky. So I call Ohio the Islamic Republic of Nohio. You cannot strip. You cannot drink. You cannot smoke, and you cannot look at young ladies who are naked. And then they wonder why Ohioans are fleeing the state!

"I had on my show Sandy Theis. She put together a group called Dancers for Democracy in which the strippers were on my show repeatedly, with their revealing tee shirts, demanding democracy. I call them the Double Ds for Democracy. The girls would come on and were wonderful guests. Most of the girls were college coeds.

"They were mainly college coeds who were literally paying their way through college making up to $1,000 a day from suckers, who were men. I think it was the men who were being exploited here. The women were not being exploited. They're making a thousand bucks a day, while these idiot men are paying twenty, forty, or fifty bucks for a bottle of beer and one hundred bucks for lousy champagne, on the condition that a half-naked women sit next to them. And the Hula Hoop Law (Willie's phrase) specifies that people must keep a six-foot distance from the dancers or strippers. If you do, you go to jail. So the strip clubs are closing down. The casinos never opened. The small clubs are shutting down, the bowling alleys are closing, all because of the smoking. And to me it is absurd. It's ridiculous. And that's why Ohio is losing jobs and has budget shortfalls because the lawmakers are real stupid."

Maybe, Willie should put down the microphone and run for Governor of Ohio on this platform.

Cunningham was once a lector at St. Gertrude Catholic Church in Madeira, where he lives. A lector reads the epistle, the prayer of the faithful. The former pastor at St. Gertrude took him aside at one point, he recalled, to relay the complaints from parishioners. "They wanted to know how in the world Bill Cunningham can be talking about sexual fantasies on Friday night and proclaiming the word of St. Paul on Sunday. I discussed that with the pastor. I said, 'Father, if Clint Eastwood plays a killer, if he rapes and kills women, would anyone say he should not be mayor of Carmel?' Of course not. If a novelist writes a story about child abuse, does that make him a child abuser? What I do on the radio is entertainment. I am here to play a role. He understands that now. In the beginning, he didn't." Well, Willie was fired as a lector nonetheless.

"My dear mother gave me roots and wings. That's what all children need," says Willie.

Willie's mother would challenge Willie. When Willie attacked the Archbishop of Cincinnati, Daniel Pilarczyk, for his handling of priest child-abuse cases, his mother thought Willie was being disloyal to Catholics. Willie defended his words by claiming the Archbishop was the problem.

"My mother was my toughest critic and greatest fan," explains Willie.

CHAPTER 31

WILLIE ON RACE ISSUES

*"I have always liked sport and only played
or ran races for the fun of the thing."*

Jim Thorpe

*D*espite Willie's work with Leslie Gaines and countless friends from the African-American communities, Willie is often accused of being a racist. He's not. He is harsh on the young black males who commit murder and abandon their children. He insists on writing this chapter. These are his words:

Cincinnati is not the national image of a race riot or an overblown racial slur by Marge Schott. Cincinnati is the greatest city in the world. Geographically, it's a short drive to Indianapolis, Chicago, Detroit, Nashville, Atlanta, Pittsburgh, St. Louis, Cleveland and Columbus. It has an annual fireworks display on its riverbanks which is unmatched. It's sponsored by Clear Channel's very own WEBN. There are casinos in Indiana nearby. There are two horse tracks. There is an arts community of plays, concerts and museums. There are great public and private schools. There are amusement parks and family parks.

There is a diversity of employment. Delta has a hub at our very own International Airport. General

Electric employs thousands. Cincinnati is home to seven Fortune 500 companies: Kroger, Proctor & Gamble, Federated Department Stores, Fifth Third Bank, Cinergy, Western & Southern Mutual and American Financial. We are also the home of Chiquita Banana. The owner of the Reds, Bob Castellini, is the largest produce distributor in the Midwest. Cintas is home here too. They are the largest uniform distributor.

The national, non-profit organization Partners for Livable Communities selected Cincinnati as "America's Most Livable City" in 2004. I call it the greatest city, in the greatest part of the greatest nation in the world — in fact, the history of the world. A little to the north is the Ohio State University, home to an overrated collegiate football team that regularly loses to the best of the SEC. A little to the north east sits the Indianapolis Motor Speedway which hosts over Memorial Day Weekend the Greatest Spectacle in Sports as well as the Richmond 400 every August. A little to the South, the winningest college basketball team of all is my Kentucky Wildcats.

Great institutions are located throughout Cincinnati such as Northern Kentucky University, University of Cincinnati, Xavier University and several smaller educational institutions such as Mt. St. Joseph, Thomas More and others. Baseball's oldest franchise, the Cincinnati Reds, is here, and one of the NFL's most woeful teams, the Cincinnati Bengals. In other words, the region in and around Cincinnati is a great place to live and work — if what I do is work. Once we were even the home of a NBA franchise, the Cincinnati Royals, which moved to Kansas City and is now the Sacramento Kings. We have had the hockey tradition of the

Cincinnati Sword, Stingers, Mighty Ducks, and National Champions – Cyclones.

Cincinnati once had a brewery on every corner. It is home to local breweries to this day. We are the creators and inventors of a meat called goetta, which many eat and most do know what its ingredients. (Goetta is a peasant food of German origin that is popular in the greater Cincinnati area. It is primarily composed of ground meat and oats, according to Wikipedia.) We are the home of the Kahn's hot dog. We once ruled the world as a pig stockyard, therefore the nickname Porkopolis. Barry Popik states that Cincinnati donned the nickname around 1843; but Chicago claimed the title in 1862. This resulted in an intercity rivalry, which resulted in the title "Windy City" going to Chicago around 1870 (http://www.barrypopik.com/index.php/new_york_city/entry/porkpolis_cincinnati_chicago_nickname/). The National Freedom Center calls Cincinnati home, as does a museum for the Underground Railroad.

Who was either born here, lived here or worked here? I say we can match this list up against *any* city's — Oscar Robertson, Ulysses S. Grant, Benjamin Harrison, Rutherford B. Hayes, James Garfield, William Howard Taft, "Mr. Republican" U.S. Senator Bob Taft, Salman P. Chase, Johnny Bench, Pete Rose, Joe Morgan, Tony Perez, Anthony Munoz, Sam Wyche, Paul Brown, Bill Walsh, Forest Gregg, Peter Frampton, Nick Lachey, Carmen Electra, Sparky Anderson, Cris Collinsworth, Tony Snow, the Crosley Brothers, Bob Trumpy, Al Michaels, E.W. Scripps, Marge Schott, Rev. Fred Shuttelsworth, Nick Clooney, George Clooney, Rosemary Clooney, Steve Cauthen, Bob Huggins, Buddy LaRosa, Skip Prosser, Ezzard Charles, Aaron Pryor,

Thad Matta, Brian Kelly, Jerry Springer, and last but not least, Larry Flynt. *Cincinnati* magazine regularly selects Willie as the most powerful person in Cincinnati media (TV, newspaper or radio).

One of the great institutions in the Tri-State region is the Cincinnati Police Division — vilified by the *Cincinnati Enquirer* and many African-Americans as a deeply troubled racist institution. In a sad way, nothing has done more for my radio career at 700WLW than the April 2001 riots that enveloped the entire city. I appeared on dozens of national television, cable and radio shows in April and May due to the so-called race riots in Cincinnati. I believed then, and I believe now, that the Cincinnati Police were crucified upon the altar of racial political correctness by left wing racial ideologies bent on attacking the centurions of freedom or bent on making millions of dollars from either the public treasury or corporate America located in or around Cincinnati.

No topic has dominated in a more consistent way than race, and all its various tentacles — touching economical, education, politics, family formation, religion and crime. Between 1996 and April 2001, Cincinnati Police killed fifteen black men. After each police shooting, my radio talk show, sadly, had a topic for next week.

The guests each time — my cast of characters were well known — Chief of Police Tom Streicher; FOP President Keith Fangman, perhaps a lawyer or two for the cops and/or the victims family and Kabaka Aba — the self appointed "General" of the Black Festival. Views split along racial lines — the great majority of my black callers mouthed the word of racial accusations against police officers, prosecutors, judges and me. Reality did not exist for them. Likewise, the great majority of my white callers viewed each of the fifteen black men killed by Cincinnati Police as "justified" due to personal misbehavior at the time of the arrest. In reality, every cop killed in Cincinnati over the last fifty years (yes, I said fifty years) was killed by a black man; and over 85 percent of assaults committed against Cincinnati cops on duty were and are committed by black men. These are horrible and disgusting facts largely ignored by the media and African-Americans — I did not ignore them.

I support cops naturally since they are the thin blue line between democracy and anarchy. So, in the five years before April 2001, the topic of racism in general and "police misconduct" in particular dominated my radio talk show like no other with a sharp diversion along racial lives. The media — print and television — generally took the side of my black callers and guests in perpetrating myths and stereotypes about policy. Beginning in 1997, the *Cincinnati Enquirer* ran repeated stories harshly criticizing Cincinnati Police. On June 27, 1997, the *Cincinnati Enquirer* ran a series of stories of police brutality in the city using a bloody photo of an African-American male screaming after an encounter with a Cincinnati cop.

Until the riots began on Monday, April 9, 2001, and through today, the *Cincinnati Enquirer* is a reliable reflection of the viewpoints of racial bigots such as leaders of the NAACP, Blacks United Front, the Black Fist and others. I will hold my breath until death to read a well-researched, front-page story reporting on why every cop in Cincinnati over the past fifty years was killed by a black man, or why cops are assaulted overwhelmingly by black men, or the dangers faced by the overwhelmingly

peaceful black community members at the hands of
young, black thugs. In reality, according to Heather
MacDonald of *City Journal* appeared on my show
to factually report that a Cincinnati cop was twen-
ty-seven more times more likely to be killed by a
black man than a black man was likely to be killed
by a Cincinnati cop. None of this ever hit the pages
of the *Cincinnati Enquirer* or local television.

Therefore, the viewpoint held by African-Americans reflected what they saw on television, read
in the *Cincinnati Enquirer*, or heard on some radio station — but not me on 700WLW. Plus, since
about 25-30 percent of young black males are convicted criminals, having been first arrested by a
cop, many blacks developed less than generous
attitudes toward cops. Historically, there may be
legitimate reasons to order a racial animus toward
cops, but not now. Having been sued, examined by
the U.S. Department of Justice, and affirmative ac-
tioned to death, Cincinnati cops alterably and ge-
netically changed in the 1980s and 90s — just like
cops around the nation. We now have great police
officers, except when they are viewed through a racial Rubik's cube.

The media gave a local rhyming reverend, Damon Lynch III, great credibility during the time by
quoting him frequently, plastering his photo on the
front page of the *Cincinnati Enquirer* and frequent
appearances on black talk radio; however, he refused to come on my talk show even one time.

The Rhyming Reverend sent out press releases
to the AP, television and radio, causing millions of
dollars in lost revenues. On my show I spoke truth
to power. Consequently, my ratings soared since
God-fearing Americans did not hear their viewpoint reflected by any organ of the media except

me. In fact, one may fairly say that my coverage of the race riots in 2001, locally, and my appearance on many national, cable and radio shows all resulted in me receiving the Marconi Award as America's Large Market Personality of the year on September 8, 2001, in New Orleans.

In 2006, Willie tried to help elect Ken Blackwell, an African-American, as Governor of Ohio. In 2008, he repeatedly called for Colin Powell, Walter Williams, or another African American like them to run for President so he could vote for them. It's not a black issue. It's a character issue for Willie. He adopts the Martin Luther King, Jr. mantra of judging by the content of character rather than the color of their skin. In 2008, Barack Obama won Hamilton County, Ohio, in the general election. It is the first time the county had voted Democrat in a Presidential election in decades. Willie's turf is changing. African-American liberals complain about the lack of blacks in more leadership positions. Perhaps the election of President Barack Hussein Obama will alter that perspective. Willie doubts it will.

CHAPTER 32

DAMON LYNCH - RIOTS

"The secret is to work less as individuals and more as a team. As a coach, I play not my eleven best, but my best eleven."

Knute Rockne

*I*n 2001, Cincinnati made national news for a riot and boycotts. "There was a riot in 2001 and it was ongoing. It was like four days of the so-called Cincinnati riots, which means no one's seriously hurt, no one's killed, no serious property damage, but it's a riot. Damon Lynch called Darryl Parks and said he wanted to meet me and Darryl Parks, the program director. I told Darryl I didn't want to go." Willie recalls.

"I'll go with you," Darryl insisted.

"At the appointed time, about two o'clock in the afternoon, Daryl and I went to 18th and Elm to see the Martin Luther King, Jr. or the Malcolm X of Cincinnati, Damon Lynch. We were in the middle of the hood, and the riots had just happened. I felt completely safe because I've been in the public defender's office for many years and I'm around blacks all the time. It didn't bother me one bit. Daryl Parks is a little antsy. So we walk into Damon Lynch's office and there's about six of the brothers standing there, and I walked in and said, 'My boys, how're you doing?' Parks was tugging on my shirt going, what the hell are you doing?

"Damon wanted to take us on a walk. Darryl stayed behind. We went out the front door, turned right, and walked three blocks," says Willie.

"I need $50 million," Damon said.

"I said, '$50 million! I could use $49 million myself.'"

"I need $50 million to redevelop this entire part of Cincinnati," he said. "Can you help me get $50 million?"

"Why don't you come on the air and talk about it?"

"Oh, I can't do that," he said.

"Just after the riots, City Council, Hamilton County and State of Ohio was throwing money at Damon Lynch. I mean, there were all these work programs, summer job programs, revitalization, urban renewal programs, but he needed $50 million," laughs Willie.

"Well, where's the money going to come from?" asked Willie.

"Well, you know all the people that live in Indian Hill."

(Indian Hill is the most well-heeled neighborhood in Cincinnati.)

I said, "I know a lot of them, but I don't know about $50 million."

"And so as we were walking, there were guys shooting craps. There was a prostitute here, a crack addict here. I thought to myself, you are Reverend Damon Lynch. You live with these people. Why don't you minister to those who need the help the most instead of trying to shake down Indian Hill for $50 million? I thought that to myself, but I didn't say it at the time. So we walked, came back. I said, 'I'll be in touch with you and see what I can do.' He said, 'Great,' and I've not seen him since," says Willie.

"There were about 1,600 lynchings in the south from the 1860s to the 1920s, 1,600 total in about seventy years, which is only a couple of weeks of killings every week in the black community. There are about 10,000 black men every year that killed 10,000 other black men. That's two hundred murders a week. After about seven weeks, you have an entire seventy years. But in the black community, a black life doesn't have value unless a white person takes it. Then there's value. Black people killing black people, there's no money to be made," explains Willie.

Willie does not have a conceal and carry license. However, he owns a .357, a Glock, and a 12-gauge shotgun. He goes to a shooting range from time to time to shoot. He believes all Americans should be armed. He believes everyone on planes and all teachers should have guns.

Willie is a Second Amendment supporter's dream.

Cries of racism will continue as long as money is paid, fame is attained, and reputations are defamed.

CHAPTER 33

RADIO GUESTS

"We must expect reverses, even defeats. They are sent to teach us wisdom and prudence, to call forth greater energies, and to prevent our falling into greater disasters."

Robert E. Lee

A nyone of note in the Greater Cincinnati area has either been in the studio or called in to be on Willie's show at one time or the other. Public officials, celebrities, business moguls, sports stars and characters of all sorts appear on Willie's show. He also has regulars like the Sheriff of Butler County, Richard Jones; Joe Deters, the Hamilton County Prosecutor; Simon Leis, the Hamilton County Sheriff; former mayor of Cincinnati, Charlie Luken; and yours truly. However, Willie has his favorites of all time.

"My three best guests of all time were James Brown, the Godfather of Soul; Charlton Heston; and Paul Harvey," said Willie.

Willie considers Paul Harvey the greatest American radio personality of all time. Harvey was born September 4, 1918. He was an American radio broadcaster for the ABC Radio Networks. He broadcasted *News and Comment* on weekday mornings and at noon on Saturdays, as well as his famous *The Rest of the Story* segments. His listening audience was estimated at 22 million people a week. Harvey is especially famous for his dramatic pauses and his voice.

In 1997, WLW's studio was in Mt. Adams. Mt. Adams is a cozy neighborhood which overlooks downtown Cincinnati on one of Cincinnati's seven hills. One day the *Mississippi Queen* steamed up the Ohio River and docked in Cincinnati for an overnight stay. On the *Queen* was Paul Harvey, his wife, Paul Harvey, Jr. and his wife. Two couples, Paul Harvey, Senior and Junior, and their wives. During the evening, the Ohio River rose eight feet, and the next day the Captain could not get the *Mississippi Queen* underneath the next bridge. So Paul Harvey and his family had to spend an extra day in Cincinnati until the river recessed. Paul Harvey hailed a cab and told the cab driver to take them to 700WLW. The cab driver brought him to the Mt. Adams studio. The Paul Harvey foursome all sported maritime linen white naval outfits. "They each have scrambled eggs on their shoulders and captain hats on. They dressed that way on their journey on the *Mississippi Queen*," Willie said.

Harvey showed up in the lobby of the building with his entourage. A young nineteen-year-old impressionable female working the front desk named Marina, a cute brunette, greeted the Harveys. Paul Harvey walked up to the front desk off the elevator and asked Marina to inform the program director that Paul Harvey was in the lobby to see him.

"Who?" she replied.

"Paul Harvey."

"Who are you with?"

"Just tell the program director — what's his name?"

"Bill Wills."

"Just tell Mr. Wills that Paul Harvey . . ."

"Sir, I have to know who you're with."

"Please just tell him that Paul Harvey is in the lobby."

She finally relented. Marina stood up and walked around the corner and down the hallway to Bill Wills' office. Wills was on the phone. Marina walked back to the front desk and informed Paul Harvey Bill Wills was on the phone right now. Paul Harvey sat down and waited. About ten minutes later, he got up and walked over to Marina.

"Would you tell the program director Paul Harvey is still here waiting for him."

"Well, he's still on the phone."

"Well then I'm going back."

"Sir, you can't do that."

"Believe me, when he sees me, he'll want to see me."

"Who are you?"

"I'm Paul Harvey."

"Young Marina had no clue who the hell Paul Harvey was," laughs Willie.

Paul Harvey and his entourage walked down the hallway to a little sign that said Program Director, and he walked into the program director's (Bill Wills') office who was still on the phone. Wills had his feet propped up on the desk, and when he looked up and saw Paul Harvey standing in his office, he could not get his feet off the desk and the phone out of his ear quick enough to welcome him. Harvey told Wills the story about the boat and the river rising and how he decided he would stop by to visit the radio station. Wills, seizing the opportunity, asked Paul Harvey if he would want to be on the Bill Cunningham show. Paul Harvey responded that he'd heard of Mr. Cunningham, and he'd love to do it.

"During a break, in walks Paul Harvey with his family in tow. They sit down and I do an hour interview with Paul Harvey. How he started in radio. How he puts his show together all the time. What is radio? Where has it been? Where is it now? Where will it be going? A great hour of radio. I got to interview the dean of radio," explains Willie. Paul Harvey is the Father of Modern Radio.

Willie's other favorite guest was James Brown, the Godfather of Soul. Brown was an American entertainer, singer, songwriter, bandleader, and record producer, who was an influential figure in 20th Century popular music. He also did the splits and spun around really well. He began his professional career in 1953 and rose to fame during the late 1950s and early 1960s. Despite personal problems and setbacks, he continued to have hits in every decade until the 1980s. During the 1960s and 1970s he became influential in American political affairs. He is known for his activist work for fellow African Americans and the poor. Also known as "The Godfather of Soul" and the "King of Funk," he played an important part in the evolution of gospel and rhythm blues into soul and funk. He laid the foundations for the music genre known as the classics of hip-hop.

"The mayor of Cincinnati at the time was Dwight Tillery. He was an African-American male who loved music and loved to honor the heritage of King Records in Cincinnati, where James Brown got his start along with Bootsy Collins. The mayor, Dwight Tillery, was running for reelection, and he had James Brown come to town to honor him and make King Records a recording studio monument," explains Willie.

"Dwight Tillery called me at noon and asked me if I would like to have James Brown on. For some reason I was thinking of the James Brown on CBS Sports. So I told Tillery, "I don't do sports that much." He said something peculiar – that he doesn't do sports either. I was puzzled. "James Brown doesn't do sports?" Tillery spoke up and explained, "James Brown, the Godfather of Soul." I said, "What? James Brown? The Godfather of Soul is in Cincinnati! Absolutely I want to have him on," Willie said.

At two o'clock on that day, in walked James Brown and his entourage to the studio. He sat down with Willie for a full hour.

"He had his cape man with him and we talked about the roots of rock n' roll and meeting Elvis Presley, how he put songs together, the racism he suffered in the south which was unbelievable in the fifties and sixties, and music. Then I was able to put the cape on James Brown at a concert he did that night, which was one of my highlights," Willie recalls.

Willie's third favorite guest was Charlton Heston. Charlton Heston played Andrew Jackson, El Cid, Moses, Ben-Hur, and he battled Apes. He won the Academy Award for best actor for *Ben-Hur*. In the 1950s and 1960s, he spoke out against racism and was an active supporter of the Civil Rights Movement. He called Willie's producer one day and said that he was at a dinner theater in Dayton, Ohio, and that he listened to 700WLW all the time when he was in the Midwest, and he wanted to see if Willie would like him to be on his show. Willie's producer was a young woman at that time.

The producer walked to the studio, swung open the door, and asked Willie, "Charlton Heston called and he wants to be on your show."

"Stop it. You don't mean Ben Hur?" Willie replied.

"Yeah, that guy."

"You're kidding me, right? Why would he want to be on my show?

"He said when he's in the Midwest, he listens."

"You tell Charlton Heston, you tell Ben Hur, you tell President Andrew Jackson, you tell Moses that if he wants to be on my show, it's a done deal!"

Charlton Heston came in at two o'clock one day and Willie spent an hour with him.

"I had done some research, and I knew all of his movie roles. We talked about him from Michelangelo to President Jackson to Ben-Hur to Moses and Planet of the Apes. A great one-hour interview with Ben-Hur. Those are my three greatest interviews, all of which came out of nowhere and weren't even planned," Willie said.

Willie also had an incoherent radio interview with Bob Hope in Hope's later years. It's hysterical. Willie and Hope are on the phone, but it sounds like neither is carrying on a conversation with the other. The producers of Willie's show often use Bob Hope's "Hello? Hello?" in "drops" during segments of Willie's show.

CHAPTER 34

DRIVING PEOPLE CRAZY

"Leaders are made; they are not born. They are made by hard effort, which is the price which all of us must pay to achieve any goal that is worthwhile."

Vince Lombardi

Today, on local radio in Cincinnati, Willie doesn't really have any competitors in talk radio. However, in 1990, Stan Solomon from WCKY thought he was. Solomon was a financial adviser and guest on WLW in the late 1980s. In 1989, he had his own radio show on WCKY. According to the January 1990 issue of *Cincinnati* magazine, Stan did not care for Willie. The following is a segment of the interview:

"Bill Cunningham is the living, breathing reality of the movie "Big", a 12-year-old in a 41-year-old body. Seriously, I think he's still searching for a pair of patent-leather shoes so he can look up girls' dresses. He attracts an audience of intellectual dwarfs. He beats watching X-rated movies, but not by much . . .

"Actually, Cunningham performs a public service. People who ordinarily would be raping, robbing, and pillaging are sitting at home, listening to him . . . He is the radio equivalent of masturbation . . .

"I wonder if he can be serious about anything. I don't think he's a bad person. I just think he's stupid, immature . . .

"You can't insult a rock. You can't insult a moron, a man with the intellectual depth of a teaspoon. Anything you say plays into his hands."

Stan Solomon soon disappeared from the local radio scene. He's now broadcasting on the Internet.

Of all ironies, the man who spewed venom about Willie became my client. I asked Willie about him, and he didn't even remember him. While Stan is on the Internet broadcasting to a miniscule audience, Willie rules the airwaves.

Willie is the master of sexual innuendo. He can push it to the edge without offending. It's part of his shtick.

"Well the reason I do sexual innuendo," Willie explained, "is that it connects with a 41-year-old male. A 41-year-old man who's been married ten to fifteen years, has a wife who probably looks like she's about forty-one years old, and has some kids. And so that guy likes sexual innuendo. He's spent his time in locker rooms, coaching his kids' teams. He's probably spent some time in a strip bar. And he probably enjoys a little bit of *Playboy* magazine now and then. So there's a way of doing it that is titillating without being sexually overt," explains Willie.

"So what I try to do when I have a young female on like former Miss America, like Heather French Henry, or some of the local news babes, all of whom are attractive with their Botox, the key is to embarrass them in such a way as to make that 41-year-old man laugh. So I do it as a way of connecting with the audience. That's why I do it, and it's entertaining. The girls tend to get embarrassed and the men like it.

"Sandra Ali and Sheree Paolello are the two news anchors at Channel 5. We had a bet or something that I won, and they had to bring me pie and warm cookies. So, on the annointed day, I looked down this long hallway and walking down is a gorgeous brunette, Sandra Ali, carrying her blueberry pie in both hands, and the other, Sheree Paolello has warm gooey cookies. So I spent the next half hour with them sampling their pie and eating their cookies, and it was hilarious. They're both very attractive, married, classy women, and they played off of it very well," said Willie.

I was in the studio that day Sandra and Sheree came in, and it is my favorite Willie moment. I laughed so hard with Willie's pie comments. At one point, Sheree Paolello turned to Sandra Ali and said, "Don't you wish you had baked him a cake?"

Another "victim" of Willie's shenanigans is Cincinnati City Councilwomen Leslie Ghiz. Elected to council in 2005, she won reelection in 2007. Willie is merciless with her. Her responses and comments are often used as "drops" during the show. She's good-humored and not stupid. She's an attorney. However, at times it's not clear whether she realizes Willie is making a joke.

It's all part of Willie's mastery as a radio entertainer.

(Above) Willie prepares to launch a 400 ft. home run.
(Below) Willie was MVP at Reds Baseball Heaven (1998).

(Above) Willie served on the Board of Trustees of Kenwood Country Club for six years.
(Below) Willie throws down with Cris Collinsworth when Cris worked at 700WLW.

Willie is led into the arena during a 700WLW program.

(Above) A listener sends Willie an annatomically-correct cake.
(Below) Willie and his radio buddy, Seg.

(Above) Willie gives Kentucky coach Rick Pitino his 44th birthday cake. (Below) Pete Rose joins Willie's basketball team.

(Above) Willie hits a 3-point "J" at Cincinnati Gardens.
(Below) Willie gets control of University of Kentucky's National Championship trophy.

Contributed photo

Contract completed

To celebrate completion of the Contract with America, Ohio 2nd District Representative Rob Portman hosted WLW talk show host Bill Cunningham at the U.S. Capitol. Cunningham broadcast his show live from the Speaker of the House's balcony recently. Guests included (shown) Speaker Newt Gingrich and Republican Conference Chairman John Boehner of the nearby Ohio 8th District.

(Above) Willie on the Portico of the US Capitol with the new speaker.

(Right) Willie (1997).

184

Dems pound at 'contract'

Hope to scare the undecided to their side

By Judy Keen
USA TODAY

Vice President Gore made it clear Tuesday the White House is in full combat mode as it braces for congressional elections on Nov. 8.

In a bare-knuckled speech to a receptive liberal audience, Gore accused Republicans of trying to "wreck Congress in order to control it, and then to wreck a presidency in order to recapture it."

He cast the elections — in which Democrats are expected to lose dozens of House seats and perhaps forfeit control of the Senate — in apocalyptic terms:

"The issue before us is not just who gains seats but whether a deliberate, protracted, reckless strategy of partisan paralysis will be permitted to stop our country's progress."

The heated rhetoric — and Gore's challenge of GOP Senate candidates Michael Huffington, Oliver North, Rick Santorum and Spencer Abraham by name — was designed to get Gore's face on TV news broadcasts.

It also revealed White House strategy for the campaign's waning days.

President Clinton is off shepherding a Middle East peace agreement, but top aides back in the White House are planning two weeks of unrelenting, no-holds-barred attacks.

Their weapon: the "Contract with America" signed by 300 Republican House candidates in September. The contract pledged a $208 billion tax cut the White House argues would result in a soaring deficit and deep cuts in education, Medicare, Social Security and other popular programs.

The contract, conceived by House GOP Whip Newt Gingrich, invigorated a White House that had been flailing for campaign ammunition.

"Newt made it easier for us to have a conversation with the voters," says White House political director Joan Baggett. "It defined the terms of the race much more clearly."

The contract "was a softball that we were praying for," says Tony Coelho, senior adviser to the Democratic National Committee.

Asked what the administration's tactic would have been without it, Coelho admits, "I don't know. We were obviously looking for what we could say to get on the offense. We were having difficulty getting the public to listen to our message."

Besides bashing the contract, administration officials will recite Clin-

POINT MAN: Vice President Gore shakes hands with Democratic supporters in Boston. Gore is leading the attack while Clinton is in the Mideast.

> **The Republicans are determined to wreck Congress in order to control it, and then to wreck a presidency in order to recapture it.**
>
> — Vice President Gore

ton's record — boasts they believe will be reinforced by images of his performance in the Middle East.

"I'll match our record vs. their contract any day," says senior Clinton adviser George Stephanopoulos.

So Gore and Clinton Cabinet members are hitting the road to blast the contract. Every Cabinet member except Attorney General Janet Reno, Secretary of State Warren Christopher and Defense Secretary William Perry is fanning out; they'll campaign in 23 states in the next 10 days.

As soon as he returns from the Middle East, Clinton also will resume campaigning: Events are scheduled in Michigan, Rhode Island, Iowa, California and Washington state.

At each stop, Clinton and his surrogates will describe their version of the contract's effect on each state. "We do want to personalize it," says Baggett.

White House strategists believe voters are only now focusing on the election and that attacks on the contract can scare those who are undecided into voting for Democrats.

They also hope their tactics will energize unenthused Democratic voters who might otherwise stay home on Election Day.

"It gave us not only a weapon to use on offense, it also gave us something to exorcise our base so that we could now go to our base and say, 'They're going after Medicare, agricultural programs,' " says Coelho.

And, perhaps most important, Clinton strategists think the contract's possible effects on the federal budget deficit will drive Ross Perot voters into the Democratic column.

"Until they introduced the contract, Republicans were able to run as the throw-the-bums-out party," says Clinton pollster Stan Greenberg.

"But when they put the contract down, they were very clear that they wanted to go back to Reagan policies. ... And people believe those times got the country in trouble," says Greenberg.

Republicans don't think any of these last-minute tactics will stave off deep Democratic losses. They're trying to neutralize Democrats' attacks on the contract by calling attention to an internal White House memo describing options for tax increases and Social Security cuts.

Republicans are convinced the election will still be a referendum on Clinton. "People's opinion of Clinton has not changed over the last few weeks: 52% disapprove. It's unprecedented," says Republican Chairman Haley Barbour. "If all politics is local, Bill Clinton's mighty unpopular — regardless of the locale."

(Above) Willie and his radio buddy, Seg.
(Below) Cartoon in the Cincinnati Post.

(Above) Willie with local leaders.
(Below) Willie meets President Bush.

To Bill Cunningham
With best wishes,

(Above) Willie, Seg and Cris Collinsworth.
(Below) Pete Rose, Willie and Hulk Hogan.

Power100

The Tristate's Most Influential People:
Who's In, Who's Out, Who's Hot, Who's Not

17 | Otto Budig Jr.

CEO AND ARTS PATRON
His family foundation continues to be the lifeblood of the arts in the region.

Top Cincy Cheerleader

NICK LACHEY
From the School for Creative and P
Arts to boy band superstars 98 Deg
MTV, Nicholas Scott Lachey, 34, em
Cincy's best celebrity promoter and
ambassador on NBC's *Clash of the*
Keep the momentum going, Nick.

18

Bill Cunningham

**TALK RADIO'S
GREATEST AMERICAN**
Without any local TV superstars, the King of WLW reigns as our leading media figure. What Willie says still becomes conventional wisdom amongst many Cincinnatians.

19 | Joe Deters

HAMILTON COUNTY PROSECUTOR
No huge victories, no major setbacks. Hamilton County's strongest Republican is well-positioned to move up the political ladder.

Willie has two Marconi's (2001 & 2009) as the Large Market American Personality of the Year.

(Above) Willie in New Orleans (2001), accepting one of his two Marconi's.
(Below) Willie and Seg with Kentucky's National Championship Trophy.

Legends of 700WLW: Jim Scott, Mike McConnell, Willie, Gary Bur-bank, Andy Furman, and Scott Sloan, with photo bust of the Truckin' Boyz (2003).

CHAPTER 35

FAMOUS PEOPLE

*"Take a method and try it. If it fails, admit it frankly,
and try another. But by all means, try something."*

Franklin D. Roosevelt

*B*eing Willie has its privileges. One of those perks is meeting
and interviewing famous people. Willie's met both President
Bushes. He's met #43 several times. He has a photograph of himself
with Rob Portman, John Boehner and Newt Gingrich. This was
taken in 1995 as the "Contract with America" swept the nation
and a new Congress was sworn in. Willie interviewed them at the
Capital where he did his radio show live. Rob Portman and John
Boehner were Cincinnati-area Congressman who were up and
coming stars in the Republican Party at the time. Newt became the
speaker. John Boehner is still the minority leader. Willie has met
Bob Dole and most the Republican brass. He had Sonny Bono on
his show at the U.S. Capital before Bono died in his skiing accident.
Sonny told Willie funny stories about Sonny and Cher.

Willie has also spoken at countless political rallies. He is close
to Sean Hannity and participated in the Hannity American Tour.
That tour raises money to send the children of soldiers who have
died, to college. Willie convinced Hannity to place Cincinnati on
the tour. Cincinnati became the smallest venue of the ones Hannity chose, but Willie came through. The event sold out at Cincinnati's Kings Island Amusement Park concert venue, Timberwolf.

Willie had met Hannity years earlier in Atlanta, Georgia.

Neil Bortz, at the time a host in Atlanta, was moving from WGSD in Atlanta to a larger station. Randy Michaels, CEO of Clear Channel, sent Willie to Atlanta to fill in between Bortz's departure and Hannity's arrival.

"Randy wanted me to go down there for a week or two and just create havoc," Willie said, "so I did and I met Hannity ten to twelve years ago." Willie and Hannity struck up a quick friendship. Both Irish, they have the same sense of humor.

"He's really a great guy, and he's always been very kind to me," Willie states gratefully. Willie appears on the *Hannity Radio Show* and *Hannity* on FOX where he always irritates liberals.

Willie has never met Rush Limbaugh. However, he did pinch-hit for him two or three times. "Randy Michaels told me Rush didn't like my act. He thought it was too entertaining. It wasn't serious enough," Willie said.

Willie is the only talk show host who beats Rush Limbaugh head to head. Rush is on the same time as Willie in Cincinnati on 55 WKRC, the Clear Channel sister station to the Big One 700WLW. Willie has two or three times the listeners of Rush Limbaugh in the time slot.

National radio and television broadcasters Boomer Esiason, Cris Collinsworth and Bob Trumpy were all 700WLW *Sports Talk* radio hosts who worked with Willie.

Boomer Esiason has a presence in the national media. He does the color for Westwood Radio and CBS Sports football games, is an analyst for ABC and HBO and replaced Don Imus on New York radio on WFAN.

Before all that, Boomer played a little football. He quarterbacked at the University of Maryland and in 1984 the Cincinnati Bengals selected Boomer in the second round of the NFL Draft. He would play for the Bengals from 1984-1992 and return in 1997 after playing several years with the New York Jets and one with the Arizona Cardinals. Boomer made it to four Pro Bowls, one Super Bowl and in 1988 was NFL MVP. In 1994, the lefty won the Walter Payton Man of the Year Award in 1995 for his charitable work. To help research to find a cure for cystic fibrosis, Boomer created the

Boomer Esiason Foundation. Boomer's son Gunner suffers from the disease.

Before Boomer ever because a national media star, he cut his teeth on 700WLW doing *Sports Talk*.

Any Cincinnati sports figure of note has been photographed with Willie: Boomer Esiason, Anthony Munoz, Johnny Bench, Pete Rose, Cris Collinsworth, Marty Brennaman, Joe Nuxhall and Buddy LaRosa. These photos can be found in his home and on the walls at Willie's Sports Café around Cincinnati. Cris Collinsworth, now of NBC, freely admits that the best job he has ever had was serving as the lead-in to Willie. Willie believes the best radio ever produced occurred when he would come in with Cris and Andy Furman early and bat around the issues of the day on 700WLW.

CHAPTER 36

NUXHALL, MARTY AND THE SEGMAN

*"It is not enough to fight. It is the spirit which we
bring to the fight that decides the issue. It's morale
that wins the victory."*

George Marshall

Willie prepares for his show by living his life. He wakes
up at 7:20 A.M. to watch CNBC. He then flips around
between FOX, CNN and *Morning Joe* on MSNBC. "I've had Joe
Scarborough on my show a lot, and I like Joe. He's a Republican
Congressman from Florida, and he's about the only conservative
on NBC. I watch the current events. I read the *Cincinnati Enquirer*.
I go on-line and I read the Drudge Report, newsmax.com, politico.
com, worldnetdaily.com, townhall.com, realclearpolitics.com. So
by the time my show arrives, if it's happened anywhere in the
world, I probably know about it. And I download from those
various web sites stories that are interesting to me if I get stuck,
or if it's a slow day or not much is going on. If nothing is going
on, you've got to make something up. So that's my show prep,"
explains Willie.

Willie is good at making up stories. One story he made up
which I believed was about Joe Nuxhall, the long time color
man for Cincinnati Reds. Joe Nuxhall was Cincinnati's own.
He is beloved by the city like no other. He's also a baseball and

broadcasting legend. On June 10, 1944, he was only fifteen when he pitched two thirds of an inning for the Cincinnati Reds in a major league game. He pitched against Stan Musial. This makes him the answer to this trivia question: Since 1901 who is the youngest player ever to play in the major leagues? Then, after his long baseball career he became "The Ol' Lefthander." He would be a broadcaster on 700WLW for the Cincinnati Reds from 1967 to 2004. He died in 2007 after a long bout with cancer. The city of Cincinnati cried.

Joe's trademark was his radio sign off — "This is the old lefthander, rounding third and heading for home." Great American Ballpark, where the Reds play, displays this phrase lit up in neon outside the stadium for everyone to see.

On June 10, 2007, the Reds honored Joe Nuxhall, Marty Brennaman, and Waite Hoyt with replica microphones that hang on the wall near the radio booth. These are the three giants in Reds broadcasting history. Marty Brennaman began his radio career with the Reds in 1974. He succeeded Al Michaels as the play-by-play announcer. He became Joe Nuxhall's partner in the radio booth. Marty called Hank Aaron's 714th career home run, Pete Rose's 4,192nd hit, Tom Browning's perfect game, Ken Griffey, Jr.'s 500th and 600th home runs, and the Reds' World Series wins in 1975, 1976 and 1990. Always outspoken and calling it straight, Marty is simply the best baseball radio announcer in the country. In 2000, he won the Ford C. Frick Award and joined baseball's Hall of Fame. At Redsfest in December, 2007 the Reds announced Nuxhall would be honored throughout the 2008 baseball season. Their uniforms displayed a dark patch with the word "NUXY" printed in white. On March 31, 2008 the Cincinnati Reds paid tribute to Nuxhall by wearing his #41 jersey for opening day.

In December 2007 and 2008 Nuxhall was named as one of the ten finalists for the National Baseball Hall of Fame's Ford C. Frick Award, an honor bestowed annually on broadcasters who make major contributions to the game of baseball. Of more than 122,000 online ballots cast by fans in 2007, Nuxhall received an astounding 82,304 votes. However, despite this incredible show of fan support, it was announced on February 19, 2008, that the Frick election committee had voted not in favor of Nuxhall, but instead the voice of the Seattle Mariners, Dave Niehaus. In 2008, Tony Kubiak won out. There is no question; Joe will be back.

On September 2004, Orange Frazer Press released a book *Joe: Rounding Third and Heading for Home*, written by Greg Hoard. A portion of the proceeds from the book benefits the Joe Nuxhall Character Education Fund, which was established in 2003 to underwrite character development programs and projects for children.

In the days following Nuxhall's death, 700WLW devoted shows to him. Fans left cards, flowers and banners at the bronze statue of Nuxhall at Great American Ball Park. A public visitation ceremony was attended by thousands of fans, and several local and national sports and broadcasting personalities. At his visitation held at Fairfield High School (Fairfield, Ohio), an estimated 6,000 people showed up to pay their respects to Nuxhall and the Nuxhall family.

Willie has told on the air several times a story about his participation in Fantasy Week during the Reds Spring Training in Florida. Men can pay money to play baseball during what is called Fantasy week at Spring Training. Willie tells how he was pitching a no-hitter perfect game. In the top of the ninth inning, his manager, Joe Nuxhall, with two outs, pulled Willie. Willie could not believe Nuxhall was ruining his perfect game. He yelled at Nuxhall. Nuxhall yelled back. They came to near blows and Nuxhall grabbed a bat and chased Willie. He tells it as truth. However, it never happened.

Willie's wingman in radio is Dennis "Segman" Dennison. 700WLW hired Segman in 1978. He began by preparing helicopter traffic reports while a student at Northern Kentucky University. He then joined the newsroom. He worked with Andy MacWilliams and Bob Trumpy in sports. Bob Trumpy gave him the nickname Segman. Segman handles 20/20 sports and hosts the *KOI Racing Report Show* Sunday night from 7-9 p.m. Segman has been at 700WLW three years longer than Willie. When Willie first began in 1983, Segman would come back from the Cincinnati Reds games and he would give Willie updates from the Reds ballpark. Willie and Segman clicked and Segman is the straight man in the duo. Willie's the comedian of the tandem.

"Segman looks like Jackie Gleason on *The Honeymooners*. He's understated, has no ego, is somewhat rotund, and eats like a condemned prisoner, but he's got a heart of gold and he knows how to play the game," assesses Willie of his sidekick.

What is called the Stooge Report is on two times, at 1:35 and 2:35 p.m. It's Segman and Willie going at it. The Three Stooges — Moe, Curly and Shemp — were brothers. They came from a small town near Brooklyn. Their last name was Horwitz. The Three Stooges began in 1934 with Columbia Studios. The Stooge Report is a take off the stooge humor. Willie's Stooge Report lasts about fifteen minutes. It's the highest rated show on 700WLW. Willie and Segman have fun and laugh. Nothing's prepared. Segman walks in just cold and Willie pounds on him. Segman doesn't respond. Segman gives Willie a shot now and then. Willie acts shocked and they move on.

"We're good buddies and he's a good man," laughs Willie.

"I can honestly say there are only two people I've worked with, in all the people I've worked with in radio, in almost thirty years, who know implicitly how to be a straight man. And one is Seg, and he says the perfect thing at the perfect time in the right number of words," says Darryl Parks.

"You'll hear the perfect pause. He has a perfect and implicit understanding of A, the performing of it and B, how to be a straight. man. Implicit understanding of it. Something that you can't teach," says Darryl Parks.

"If you really listen to the Stooge Report, and this is a credit to Willie, Willie makes fun of Seg and calls him a bo-bo and calls him all these names. And at the end of every Stooge Report, the characters are out of face. Seg is the common sense guy and Willie is the bo-bo," explains Darryl Parks.

"And what that does is it takes the edge off of Willie. With many of the very difficult things, hard things and difficult topics that are discussed, Willie is a good enough entertainer to realize, and to know, that it's okay to poke fun at himself. And those characters are knocked out of face at the end of that bit. And it takes the edge off the show is what it does." explains Darryl Parks.

For Segman, 700WLW is his life. He lives there.

"I'm going to hate it when he leaves. He just turned fifty. He started here out of college at NKU when he did an internship. There was a note on the bulletin board for an intern, sports intern, at WLW and he started at that point. He has spent his entire life here. He works seven days a week, 364 days a year. He does not work on Christmas. He works every other day. And if he had put that much time into Procter & Gamble, he'd be rich. But instead, he earns a nice living. It's his entire life, and he's a radio man through and through," explains Willie.

Danny Gleason served as Willie's producer for seven years. He was very adroit at playing the "drops" and the comments at the right time. Matt Steinman is at the controls now. There are about forty drops from famous people with short little three-second bits that have to be played quickly and appropriately based upon whatever Seg and Willie happen to say. Gleason, and now Steinman, are wonderful at the task.

"Gleason wasn't the original guy doing it. The original guy doing it was a fellow named Brian Perry. Brian put together some pretty funny stuff, and then Danny took over and Danny developed a lot of the sound bites," said Darryl Parks.

Willie's current producer Matt Steinman is "affectionately" referred to by Willie as Matt "Steinkopf."

It's always a honor to be selected as the Third Stooge. This is just Willie's inviting someone on to interface with him and Segman. I've done it several times and it's a great time. Willie's buddy Andy Furman and former Cincinnati Mayor Charlie Luken are the two best third stooges.

CHAPTER 37
RADIO SHTICK

"Fame is like a shaved pig with a greased tail, and it is only after it has slipped through the hands of some thousands, that some fellow, by mere chance, holds on to it!"

Davy Crockett

The *Cincinnati* magazine (January 1990) did an exposé on Willie and called him the "silver-tongued devil." Willie, in the article, explained that to succeed in the talk show business, one needs to be confrontational or humorous. The magazine called him "quick-witted, antagonistic, foul-mouthed, and popular."

Willie believed being a lawyer helped him be a talk show host because he was trained to be quick on his feet. I call it knowing how to "dance."

Willie has never been sued for radio conduct. He's also avoided trouble with the FCC. His ratings are always great. Willie did duck a lawsuit from former Reds baseball player Adam Dunn. A former standout high school quarterback at Texas (Texas High School), Dunn signed with the University of Texas. However, Dunn quit football and concentrated on baseball. The Reds drafted Dunn in the second round of the 1998 amateur draft while he was still an active collegian. Dunn signed with the Reds and quit college.

Dunn made his Major League debut on July 20, 2001, and set a National League rookie record for the most home runs in a month by hitting twelve in August. On September 30, 2004, Dunn once again got his name in Major League Baseball's record book albeit not in the manner he wished. That day, Dunn struck out three times against Chicago Cubs right hander Mark Prior, raising his season total to 191 and surpassing Bobby Bonds' single season strikeout record of 189, set in 1970. He finished the season with 195 strikeouts. Later Ryan Howard struck out 199 times in the 2007 season.

Dunn's 46 long balls in 2004 were the fourth most in Cincinnati Reds history. That year, he joined Hall of Fame second baseman Joe Morgan as the only Reds players to score 100 runs, drive in 100 runs, and draw 100 walks in a single season. Dunn repeated the feat the following season, making him the only player in Reds history to do it more than once.

On October 31, 2007, the Reds picked up Dunn's $13 million dollar option, making him the highest-paid player on the team. The Reds traded him in 2008. In 2008, Willie made a comment about Dunn playing like a drunken softball player. Dunn was not too amused. Willie had to go apologize to him. Dunn never accepted the apology.

Darryl Parks understands talk radio and Willie's ability to execute. "Willie is the quintessential entertainer on the radio. I was talking to somebody one time and they said they were talking about looking for more depth in content," said Darryl.

"Do you consider me a serious person?" I said to them.

"Yeah."

"Well, would it surprise you to know that I would always go for the sizzle before content?"

"Yeah. Why?"

"Well I can teach anybody how to do a talk show. As far as being an entertainer, I cannot teach that. That's ingrained."

And being an entertainer is first and foremost what Willie is.

"I think talk show hosts get caught up in agendas. For example, they think their job is to change one liberal mind to a conservative every day," said Darryl.

"If that's your agenda, you will lose every time. It is all about making people react — making them cry, laugh, and think — about entertaining people. I mean, why do people go to horror movies or to see Halloween 43 now? Why are you going to do that? It's an escape. You are not going there to laugh, but you're going there to be entertained. It is escapism and radio is escapism. Radio is also about affirmation. It's community. WLW is about a community. And the longevity of all the hosts on WLW bring to the party that affirmation, that familiarity. I've make the statement, everybody's been here for twenty-five years. That's the good news. The bad news is everybody's been here for twenty-five years. I say to Willie all the time we have to think about 2015. We were talking one day and I said, "2015's here. It came a little bit early. We have to prepare for changes with people retiring or what have you."

CHAPTER 38

DARRYL AND WILLIE GO TO WASHINGTON

"A zeal for the defense of their country led these heroes to the scene of action, though with a few men to attack a powerful army of experienced warriors."

Daniel Boone

*D*arryl and Willie once went to the Pentagon in Washington, D.C. where they planned on broadcasting from the courtyard of the Pentagon on a Sunday. They were inspired by 9/11. The Pentagon was constructed from 1941 to 1943. It covers 29 acres and 17.5 miles of corridors. The Army Corps of Engineers built it in only sixteen months. Can you imagine that happening today? Of course, not. The Pentagon houses the Department of Defense. Currently, 23,000 employees work there. It is 3,705,793 square feet.

On September 11, 2001, American Airlines Flight 77 crashed into the west side of the Pentagon. Over a hundred people in the Pentagon died.

Darryl and Willie decided to catch some football before the Pentagon show.

"I want to watch the Bengals game," said Willie

"Okay," said Darryl.

"We have to find a sports bar."

"I know where there's one."

They drove to the ESPN Zone, parked the car and walked in and approached the hostess stand.

"Oh, no, you have to give your name down at the end of the stairs," said a young woman.

"How long is the wait?" asked Darryl.

"Forty-five minutes."

"Okay, that's not bad."

Darryl and Willie walked back downstairs, went to the next hostess stand and gave their names.

"We'd like a table near a screen with the Bengals game," said Darryl.

"Well, that'll be about a three hour wait."

"They just said forty-five minutes upstairs."

"Three hours."

Darryl told Willie they should go to the bar.

"Sooner or later somebody is going to leave at the bar and we can sit down and grab a burger."

"Okay," said Willie

They stood by the bar. The Bengals were playing Kansas City. It would be the game where the Chiefs' quarterback, Trent Green, would be seriously injured. After five minutes, Darryl saw Willie pull out a twenty dollar bill. Willie had been fidgeting and was impatient as always.

"I'm going to take care of this right now," said Willie.

Willie walked up to the manager. A few seconds later, Willie returned with the twenty back in his pocket.

"Well, obviously, the twenty failed to get his attention," said Willie.

"What was your first clue Willie? Washington, D.C.?" laughs Darryl.

When Darryl and Willie arrived at the Pentagon, they were supposed to go in one entrance and they couldn't find it. The building is massive. They followed the written directions given, but they were still lost. No one answered at the group of doors.

"Nobody's here, Willie."

Willie banged on the doors. "Let me in," he said. "Cunningham here."

"Willie. What are you doing?"

Willie seemed to think someone at the Pentagon would care that "Cunningham" was there.

They began to walk around the building. Darryl dragged equipment as they walked. Willie was oblivious to it. They finally found their entrance. They walked up a stairs where a walkway passed over a driveway to security. There were two points of security. As they approached the first point, the guard said from twenty-five feet away. "Hey, are you Cunningham?"

"You've got to be kidding me. How does he know you?" Darryl said to Willie.

"I have no idea."

Willie answered the guard, "Yeah, I'm Bill Cunningham."

The guard had seen Willie as a guest on *Hannity & Colmes*.

Willie and the guard expressed a few pleasantries, and Darryl and Willie did their show with the knowledge at least one person at the Pentagon knew "Cunningham."

Chapter 39

Friends and Fun

"Do not pray for easy lives. Pray to be stronger men."

John F. Kennedy

Willie is a very good friend. He's also low maintenance. However, like everyone, he doesn't have time for a lot of friends. Cicero, the great Roman Senator, lawyer and orator during the Republic, wrote a treatise on friendship. One of his commentaries involved how we do not have time for a lot of friends. Willie doesn't either. I talk to him almost every day. We each get to the point of the call and move on. I respect his time and he respects mine. The interview for this book involved the longest time I've spent with him — a few hours each day for three days. He laid on my couch in my office and answered the questions lying down in comfort. It was classic Willie.

Mark Menke is one of Willie's buddies. "I met Billy in 1975, I guess," Menke said. "He had just come back from Toledo. My younger brother was the assistant golf pro at Sharon Woods, and we played golf there. Bill drove up in a big, white Imperial, a dinosaur of a car. He had a cowboy hat on. Throws open the door and screams out, 'Does anybody want to play golf for money?' I like this guy, I said to myself. So that was the beginning of the friendship." The scene conjures up the scene of Rodney Dangerfield in *Caddyshack* where Rodney takes over the golf course to the chagrin of Ted Knight.

I've been on the river all my life, and I had an offshore power boat. Penny called us the hombres. We'd go boating, and I always told him, I said "You don't understand these police down here on the river. They take no guff, nothing," Menke said.

"Don't worry about it; I can handle them," Willie replied.

"A couple weeks later, sure enough, here come the boat police. I told Willie to be quiet. They pulled up and informed us they were going to board our vessel. As they got on. Willie said 'God Bless America. I'm the voice of the common man. I'm Bill Cunningham.' I about died," Menke said.

"Sir, are you the pilot of this boat?" the woman officer said to Willie.

"No, I'm not. He is," replied Willie.

"Well, then you sit down and shut up."

"Willie sat down, crossed his arms, and shut up," laughs Mark.

"Another good one is when we were down in the Bahamas. Penny and Bill were married at the time, and Evan was there too. Bill is a brilliant man, but if you tell him to do something with his hands, he doesn't understand. We rented mopeds to ride around the island. They have a centrifugal clutch where you give it a little gas and it starts to spin and it slowly pulls away. Well, Bill gave it gas and it wouldn't move. I told Billy to just give it a little gas. Well, he cracked it wide open, the clutch grabbed, and he shot out like a cannon into a taxi-cab door. He totaled his moped. So he got on the back of mine. I said, 'Well, hopefully not too many people saw that, the two of us riding around the Bahamas on a moped.'

"In Fort Myers, back in the late eighties, Fiddlesticks was one of the premier country clubs. I had access to it. We played golf in the morning, and then we went out on my boat off Sanibel Island. Bill almost drowned as a kid, so he's not real fond of water.

"We were hanging out off Sanibel Island in my boat. We got out, and we couldn't see land. No waves, no nothing. Very calm, very quiet. I lay on the raft and splashed water, having a big time, and he wouldn't get in. He sat on the back of the swim platform dangling his feet in the water. He went off on a God Bless America speech: 'Isn't life grand?'

"And he kind of cocked his ear," Mark recalled.

"Do you hear that?" Willie asked.

"No. What are you talking about?" I inquired.

"I hear a motor."

"Oh there's a boat out on the horizon."

"We couldn't see anything other than that boat. In twenty minutes it pulled up to us. Three guys were on it, and the guy up in the tuna tower hollered down for us to get out of the water and leave the area."

Bill and I looked up at him.

"What's the problem?" asked Mark.

"We're tarpon fishing in the area and I said you're scaring the fish."

"Sorry, sir, didn't mean to bother you, "I'm getting out of the water. I will be getting in my boat and we will be leaving."

Willie looked at Mark in bewilderment. We started up and headed back.

"Why did you do that?" asked Willie.

"Bill, there's nothing around. This boat out of nowhere comes over and tells us to leave. Put two and two together. There's a plane going to come over here and something is going to get pushed out of the side of it and they don't want us around. Why else?"

Willie has honesty and integrity. I always say if you do not commit crimes, are honest and don't steal, your enemies will never get you. The government will not either. Mark Menke recalls how Willie's honesty saved his neck.

He had a friend who was big in the Democratic party at the time. Willie was a Democrat. That is how many years ago it was. We had to give a thousand dollars each to this guy, and he was going to smooth the waters for us to get a liquor license. I had to become a Democrat too," laughs Mark.

"My poor grandmother is still rolling in her grave. But I became a Democrat and gave the money and one thing led to another. It all fell through. But a year and a half later, through this guy, Willie did get part of a license."

"We became third owners of the place where they sell license plates and driver's license and all that. Bill received a cash envelope every month. He asked me what to do. I told him to claim it. Well, after a couple of years, suddenly some light got shined on the guy and the government checked on Willie and another partner involved in it. Bill claimed his money on his taxes. The other two didn't," recalls Mark.

"Willie loves to play golf and he's a scratch golfer. He plays with guys he calls the Great Barrosik and the Flying Tunas, his best buddies. Hell, I have no idea what their real names are.

"I'll take him as a partner anytime, anywhere. He has the knack; if you back him into the corner, he'll always find a way out. The man can get up and down out of a garbage can. He's one of the best putters ever. He's got an excellent touch," said Mark.

"I don't know where he's at now, but he's been close to a scratch. Willie doesn't hang out. Willie wants to play golf, play for the money, done. Thank you, bye. He won't hang out at the country club. He hates mingling. Give him his close friends, and he'll stay out and hang. But no back slapping; he hates it. Hates it," Mark explained.

Willie began a tradition of wearing a yellow sport coat every time he appeared on *Hannity & Colmes*. The other talk show hosts at the radio station began teasing Willie about the coat. It certainly did not provide Willie a GQ look.

In response, live on the radio, Willie told the story of how he came to own the coat. He said his son, Evan, gave him the coat at Christmas; Evan had saved money year after year. The story, as it went on, brought a tear to even the hardened listener. Next, Willie asked the listeners to vote on an online poll. Should the coat go or stay? Over the course of several days, the listeners voted, and Willie's coat was saved.

Evan received calls expressing heartfelt comments about his gift. There was one issue: it never happened.

"I never gave him the coat. Completely fabricated. He had me on the air. I had no clue what he was talking about," Evan said.

"Billy called Evan because he knew Evan hadn't done it," Penny said, laughing. "We bought that coat. Billy does that once every couple of years; he buys all the pants, shirts and jackets," explains Penny.

Remember the song from James Taylor, *Up on the Roof*? Willie has a up on the roof story.

In August 2007, Willie, at Penny's request, climbed up on the roof of his house to clean the gutters. It was a mistake. Willie is scared of heights. Once on the roof, Willie suffered an anxiety attack and he had to use his cell phone to call the fire department. The radio station secured his 911 call and enjoyed playing it on the air. A frightened Willie is heard explaining his predicament. The 911 operator asked if he was the radio talk show host. She chuckled on the phone. The fire department came to Willie's home with sirens blaring and lights flashing and, to his utter embarrassment, the firefighters helped him down.

Willie can find fun and entertainment in any situation.

Willie had a misadventure one day at home which resulted in the toilet seat breaking off the bowl. Evan came up with the idea for Willie to raffle off the toilet seat to raise money for a good cause. Willie took the toilet seat to the radio station, placed a photo of it on the website, and began promoting bidding for the benefit of Madeira High School.

I was the highest bidder until someone from out of town outbid me and won the sought-after prize. I had planned to place a photo of Willie and me in the middle and use the seat as a frame.

The winning bid was around $500. If only we would have thought of just sending the toilet seat to Keith Olbermann.

CHAPTER 40

JOHN "WAYNE" MCCAIN OR "JUAN PABLO" MCCAIN

*"Live is not a spectator sport. If you're going to spend
your whole life in the grandstand just watching what
goes on, in my opinion you're wasting your life."*

Jackie Robinson

*I*n the fall of 2007, Republican presidential candidates stood
on stage after stage and debated.

"Nine men sought the nomination. McCain, in my opinion, was
number ten. I didn't like his political philosophy at all. He is a liberal Republican like a Nelson Rockefeller or a Bob Packwood. He
hooked up with Ted Kennedy. He did a deal with Russ Feingold.
He did a deal with Joe Lieberman. He opposed drilling in ANWR.
He is against water boarding. He wanted to shut down Gitmo,
and he wanted to give amnesty to illegals. That sounds like Ted
Kennedy," Willie ranted.

John McCain, born August 29, 1936, graduated from the United
States Naval Academy in 1958. He became a naval aviator and flew
missions from aircraft carriers during the Vietnam War. In 1967, he
almost died in a fire on the USS Forrestal. Later in the same year,
he was shot down while flying a mission. The North Vietnamese
captured him, severely injured. For five and half years, they held
him as a prisoner and tortured him. After his release, he worked
in Washington, D.C. for the Navy.

He retired from the Navy in 1981 and won a seat to the House of Representatives from Arizona in 1982. He jumped to the Senate in 1986. He survived the Keating Five scandal of the late 1980s. He earned a reputation as a maverick, for being a moderate, and being a compromiser by working with Democrats to pass legislation. In 2000, he lost the Republican nomination for President to George W. Bush.

In the middle of February 2008, the McCain campaign wanted McCain to come on Willie's radio show. A surrogate, former U.S. Senator from Ohio, Michael DeWine called on Willie. The idea was to insure a "softball" interview before the Ohio primary. Willie agreed to meet DeWine, one of McCain's Ohio chairmen, and Joe Deters, Hamilton County Prosecutor, and a county coordinator for McCain at P.F. Chang's restaurant in Norwood, Ohio.

The table talk focused on Willie's opinion of McCain. Willie told Senator DeWine his issues with McCain. DeWine argued with Willie about McCain's "right" position on the surge in Iraq, abortion and earmarks to counter Willie's "liberal" concerns.

"He brought up every point to counter-balance McCain as a liberal. So, after a couple of wonton soups and lettuce wraps, I agreed to have him on my show the day before the Ohio primary," said Willie.

The next day, Willie received a call from Joe Deters informing him of a big rally for McCain on February 26, 2008. Joe asked Willie to warm up the crowd with some "red meat." Former Ohio Congressman and Bush Cabinet member Rob Portman would introduce McCain. Willie would speak before Portman.

"What do you want me to say Joe?," asked Willie.

"Just do what you normally do," responded Joe.

"Well, I can do what I normally do. I'll do it."

The event was planned for Memorial Hall in the Over-The-Rhine section of Cincinnati. The forum holds a couple of hundred people. It would not be an Obama stadium fest. The claim to fame of Memorial Hall is that it is the resting place of the funeral flowers of Abraham Lincoln's casket as it came through Columbus, Ohio. The building, constructed in the middle 1800s is beautiful. A few days before the McCain rally, which held two hundred coerced, ticketed supporters, Barack Hussein Obama held an overflow rally before 15,000 screaming Obama maniacs at the University of Cincinnati. Willie knew then McCain was in trouble.

As usual, Willie prepared no written remarks. The campaign told Willie to keep looking to his side as he spoke so he could be given either a stretch or cut sign based upon where DeWine and McCain were on their route to the hall. Willie went to the event by himself. Joe Deters introduced Willie. Joe called Willie "The Voice of the Common Man" and a "great Republican."

"I actually take offense to that because I'm a great American who happens to be Republican," laughs Willie.

Willie walked out on stage after Deters' introduction. About five to six minutes in his speech, Willie looked to his right and Joe Deters gave Willie the stretch sign. Willie made a few remarks about Barack Hussein Obama being part of the Chicago Daley political machine. Willie called Obama a hack. He spoke of the federal criminal indictment of Tony Rezko. "I told the crowd the Clinton-estas would take the bark off the Obama tree," said Willie.

Willie mocked the Illinois Senator's foreign policy statements about his willingness to meet with the leaders of rogue nations. He said he envisioned a future in which "the great prophet from Chicago takes the stand and the world leaders who want to kill us will simply be singing *Kumbaya* together around the table with Barack Obama."

Willie compared Secretary of State Condoleezza Rice to Madeleine Albright, whom he said "looks like death warmed over." He also commented on the difference between former Ohio Rep. Rob Portman, whose wife is Jane, and Massachusetts Rep. Barney Frank, an openly gay member of Congress. "Jane's the main difference. But that's a different story, Willie said.

"At some point in the near future the media, the stooges from the New York Times, CBS (The Clinton Broadcasting System), NBC (The Nobody But Clinton Network), The All Bill Clinton Channel (ABC), and the Clinton News Network at some point is going to peel the bark off Barack Hussein Obama," he continued.

Willie proved a fortuneteller because after the Reverend Jeremiah Wright speeches came out, the bark was peeled.

Willie, after a stretch sign, spoke about John "Wayne" McCain, the tiger cages of the Hanoi Hilton and McCain's bravery. Willie had to keep the material coming. Willie was cooking a home stew to hungry politicos.

"I look over the crowd of 200 to 300 people, and they were applauding and screaming. The crowd contained only invitees of the Hamilton County Republican Party or the McCain campaign. No protestors. No Democrats." said Willie.

Willie noticed a group of television cameras, microphones and photographers. The platform where they rested was only twenty feet in front of him. Willie recognized a few of the faces of national reporters. However, Willie assumed they were just waiting for the main entrée, John McCain and could care less about his remarks. Willie was only an appetizer. Willie continued his normal Barack Hussein Obama rant. He used Obama's middle name three times. Willie looked to his right and Joe Deters finally gave him the "stop sign" of a slash across the throat. On cue, Willie wrapped up his remarks. Willie then headed to the Big One 700WLW to do his afternoon show.

CHAPTER 41

ALL HELL BREAKS LOOSE

"Yesterday is not ours to recover, but tomorrow is ours to win or lose."

Lyndon B. Johnson

Willie arrived at the radio station and began his show. As soon as the George Thorogood "Bad to the Bone" introduction was over, Willie launched into the glorious past of John "Wayne" McCain, that he was an important leader for America and that he was a man of character, promise and virtue. Willie was doing more than promoting John McCain.

Radio callers to WLW know the number by heart: (513) 749-7000. It is repeated countless times over a 24-hour period. As a substitute talk show host for the station, I have repeated the number so many times; I can say it in my sleep. However, for friends, family and other "very important people," there is a line called the celebrity hotline. I will not reveal the number out of fear it would be abused by a regular caller known as Nick from Fairfield. An hour and a half into Willie's show, the celebrity hotline rang. It was Joe Deters. Willie and Joe spoke off the air.

"Willie, you caused a firestorm down here."

"What you mean?"

"You said his full name three times," Deters said.

"I said his name three times. So?"

"I'm serious," Deters said.

"What's the firestorm?" Willie inquired.

216

"The media there didn't like you using his middle name, Hussein. They felt that it was racially motivated and intended to ridicule him."

Joe gave the WLW news department the words of John McCain castigating Willie for engaging in dirty politics. A reporter told McCain that Willie "denigrated" Obama and Clinton.

"I didn't denigrate anyone. I stated the facts," insisted Willie. "Joe, what does this mean?" he asked.

"You could be in big trouble with the media."

"Well, that's not unusual for me. What am I supposed to do?"

"I don't know. I just wanted to let you know a firestorm is brewing."

When Willie left the airwaves, messages waited for him from NBC, ABC, CNN, FOX, MSNBC, AP, and all four local television stations asking for his reaction to what McCain said about him.

"I apologize for it. I did not know about these remarks, but I take responsibility for them. I repudiate them. My entire campaign I have treated Senator Obama and Senator Clinton with respect. I will continue to do that throughout this campaign," McCain had told reporters.

McCain called both Democrats "honorable Americans" and said, "I want to dissociate myself with any disparaging remarks that may have been said about them."

Asked whether the use of Obama's middle name, the same as former Iraqi leader Saddam Hussein was proper, McCain said: "No, it is not. Any comment that is disparaging of either Senator Clinton or Senator Obama is totally inappropriate."

McCain said he didn't know who decided to allow Willie to speak, but he said he was sure it was in coordination with his campaign. He said he didn't hear the comments and has never met Cunningham, but "I will certainly make sure that nothing like that happens again."

Responding to McCain's apology, Obama spokesman Bill Burton said, "It is a sign that if there is a McCain-Obama general election, it can be intensely competitive, but the candidates will attempt to keep it respectful and focused on issues."

As Willie had finished his remarks at Memorial Hall, Rob Portman, who was once mentioned as a possible vice presidential candidate for McCain, took the microphone to introduce McCain.

"Willie, you're out of control again. So, what else is new? But we love him. But I've got to tell you, Bill Cunningham lending his voice to this campaign is extremely important. He did it in 2000; he did it in 2004. It was crucial to victory then and it is even more important this year with his bigger radio audience. So, Bill Cunningham, thank you for lending your voice," said Portman.

When Portman spoke to reporters later, standing next to McCain, he changed his tune.

"I was backstage so I didn't hear everything he said. Bill Cunningham is a radio talk show host who is often controversial. That's, I guess, how he makes his living." Portman flipped on Willie to curry favor with McCain.

When Willie listened in the newsroom to McCain's remarks, he could not believe what he heard. "He was mean. He was sarcastic. And he was wrong," said Willie.

Over the next twenty-one hours, before Willie was on the air again, he held dozens of interviews. Willie's objective was to publicize the fact he be allowed to say the full name of a candidate running for President. "I told these media outlets, John Fitzgerald Kennedy, Franklin Delano Roosevelt, Ronald Wilson Reagan, William Jefferson Clinton, and Hillary Rodham Clinton. Those are names given in respect to a person running. I said the name, Barack Hussein Obama three times. My goal was to identify the person to show respect to the high office to which he was seeking. That was my goal. I've used that name for four years," insists Willie.

The sensitivity of the national media and McCain, in erasing Obama's middle name, is indicative of political correctness and, at the time, it confirmed Willie's belief that America is not ready for a "black" President since all politicians should be governed by the same rules. Events reflected the "ready" belief.

Sean Hannity, on *Hannity & Colmes*, defended Willie. John Roberts of CNN and MSNBC interviewed Willie and seemed to enjoy

Willie's attack on McCain. Willie was angry because John McCain had "thrown him under the bus." John McCain didn't hear Willie's entire speech and did not realize that Willie had done as he had been asked, and McCain, like Peter denying Jesus, denied having met or heard of Willie.

Willie responded, "I'd met McCain a couple times, and he was on my show several times." Willie, at Senator DeWine's invitation, had met McCain at a dinner at the Kenwood Country Club. "I told DeWine that McCain was not my favorite candidate, but I said, 'He's a Senator, I'll meet him.'" Willie spoke to McCain at the event for a while. "We spoke politics, talk radio, Ted Kennedy and life in general" Willie said.

On another occasion, Robert Rhein, a homebuilder and developer, had called Willie at his home. Rhein too belongs to the Kenwood Country Club. Rhein asked Willie to come to a fundraiser at Rhein's house.

"You don't have to pay," said Rhein.

"Well, I can't pay to go to a fundraiser," Willie said.

"I'd like you to come and meet the Senator."

Willie went. Now, why would Senator DeWine and Robert Rhein want Willie to meet McCain? Because Willie is the number one talk show host, on the number one radio station right smack in the middle of the Midwest. They weren't stupid.

McCain also appeared on Willie's radio show three or four times. Once was in person, the others by phone.

"In January 1995, the Republicans seized power with Newt Gingrich and John Boehner, U.S. Representative from Butler County. I set my show up on the portico of the Speaker of the House which overlooks the Washington Monument. It's beautiful. I am the only radio talk show host in America ever given that honor. They set up interviews in the Senate and the House. And McCain was one of the people on the show, along with Santorum, Gingrich, Dole, Sonny Bono, and a bunch of other politicos. It was set up by John Boehner's office. So I met McCain there. I had him on by phone two or three times when he wrote his book *Faith of Our Fathers*; but it doesn't surprise me he doesn't remember. He probably meets a hundred people like me. I was always kind to him because he's an American hero. Hell, he was tortured for five and a half years," explains Willie.

John McCain was making a mistake that would cost him Ohio and the Presidency.

CHAPTER 42

THE HELL KEEPS GOING

"Those who dare to fail greatly can achieve greatly."

Bobby Kennedy

Willie continued his interviews into the next several days. "I did FOX on Neil Cavuto and *Hannity & Colmes*, and they replayed it. CNN replayed it all day. I did an interview with the AP, and that interview went out all over the country to all the newspapers," recalls Willie.

"I did all the local television news: 5, 9, 12, and 19. And then the next day, which would have been a Thursday, ABC Radio and NPR. But every ten minutes, for two and a half hours, I did ten-minute wheel interviews around the country with a different radio station, and I probably did thirty or forty of those, all on the issue of Barack Hussein Obama," Willie said.

"No questions were asked about Tony Rezko. The focus of the interview was not about Rezko, about the $300,000 deal Barack Hussein Obama got. Nothing about illegal loans, nothing about the $150,000 Rezko gave to Barack in exchange for political favors. The whole focus of all the interviews was Barack Hussein Obama. 'Your motivation was what? You had to have known this was going to cause a reaction. Are you joining an anti-Muslim fury around the nation? Is it a hate crime to call him Barack Hussein Obama?'"

"I spent the next week fending off charges that I have an anti-Muslim bias, that I'm anti-American, and I'm part of dirty politics.

Nobody complained that one word I said in that ten minutes was false. That was the whole thing. And I couldn't believe it. Nobody from Ireland was mad that I said John Fitzgerald Kennedy," said Willie.

Willie admits to one honest mistake the first week in January. He had read on a web site that Barack was born Barack Mohammed Hussein Obama, and he mentioned that.

Barack Hussein Obama was born to a Kenyan father and white American mother. He spent most his childhood in Honolulu, Hawaii. At age six, he moved to Jakarta, Indonesia, where he lived with his mother and Indonesian stepfather. A graduate of Columbia University and Harvard Law School, Obama worked as a community organizer, professor and lawyer. He served in the Illinois State Senate from 1997 to 2004.

He ran unsuccessfully for the U.S. House in 2000. He won a U.S. Senate seat in 2004. Prior to that general election victory, he delivered the keynote address at the Democratic National Convention.

Willie said the Mohammed remark on the air only three or four times because he received some e-mails and somebody sent him a copy of Barack's birth certificate from Hawaii. Willie stopped using Mohammad and apologized on the air. "My name is William

Daniel Cunningham, if somebody would call me William Patrick Daniel Cunningham, I wouldn't get my boxers in a bunch," laughs Willie. Willie has also laid off the birth certificate issue.

Jim Borgman was the cartoonist at the *Cincinnati Enquirer* at the time. The next day, Wednesday, February 27, Borgman drew McCain speaking to a reporter: "I've reconsidered my position on torture." Willie is seen hanging over sharks. It was funny, and, as good comics often do, captured it all with a drawing. Borgman had featured Willie before in his cartoons.

"Every time, I was shown in a negative way. I think in the mid-1990s I said I might run for the Congress of the United States. It was around Christmastime, and Borgman did a cartoon which had a goofy caricature of me and a commentators off to the side saying, 'The fruitcakes arrive early for Christmas,' referring to me as a fruitcake," says Willie with little humor.

It is difficult for a Republican politician to win Ohio in a Presidential election without Willie's vocal endorsement. No Republican has won the White House without winning the swing state of Ohio. McCain kept the record intact.

CHAPTER 43

MAYOR MALLORY THROWS ANOTHER WILD PITCH

"If a man hasn't discovered something that he will die for, he isn't fit to live."

Martin Luther King, Jr.

Cincinnati Mayor Mark Mallory made the national news by throwing the Cincinnati Reds 2007 Opening Day pitch somewhere between the on-deck circle and the dugout. In 2006 when he ran for mayor, his opponent was David Pepper. Mallory, black, and Pepper, white, made for a close contest. Both were Democrats with impressive lineage. Pepper's father, John Pepper, was the CEO of Cincinnati-based international consumer products giant, Proctor & Gamble. Mallory's brother, William, is a Hamilton County Judge, and his father, also William, served over twenty years in the Ohio legislature. I attended and graduated Chase Law School with the Judge. The Mallory and Pepper families are both great Cincinnati families

William Sr. and William Jr. both asked Willie to support Mark for mayor. Willie met with Mark a few times and concluded he was a reasonable man, so Willie endorsed him. Mallory is also a sharply dressed man. He's always wearing a nice suit and tie. The race for Mayor was close and, because of that, Willie believes his words of support were worth a few votes. After and since his election, Willie's had the Mayor on the air a few times.

Willie helped elect Mayor Charlie Luken by having him on his show dozens of times. In one notable call to Charlie's home, the Mayor's son, Sam, answered the call. At that time Sam was ten years old. He related that his dad and mom were out for the night. Unbeknownst to Sam, his father and mother were listening in the car as their son began answering probing question such as — Does your dad whip you? If you are bad, does your dad lock you in the closet? On and on, Willie quizzed Sam about intimate aspects of family life. Before the days of cell phone use, the mayor was speechless and helpless.

On the day of the McCain controversy, Mayor Mallory was scheduled to call Willie on the air to talk about Obama in preparation for Ohio. Mallory was a Democrat super delegate. The next nearest super delegate was in Dayton, Ohio. Mallory had earlier introduced Hillary Clinton at an event at a Skyline Chili restaurant a few days before in Cincinnati.

"After the Clinton event, Barack Hussein Obama appeared at the Fifth Third Arena at the University of Cincinnati. Mallory introduced Barack Obama and pledged his support him. Mallory was the guy designated by the Obama campaign to come on my show. He was supposed to have been on at two, but like a typical Democrat, he was way late. He called at 2:45. Republicans, in the last fifteen years on my show, almost all call on time. If it's a Republican, if I ask them to be there at 2:05 — and I've had on all the big ones — they're there at 2:05. In fact, a minute early. If it's a Democrat, whether Clinton's running, Gore, Kerry, doesn't make any difference; Democrats are always late and Republicans are always on time. This Democrat was scheduled at 2:06 Eastern time. He called at 2:45. Just so happens that we were available," said Willie.

Willie put Mallory on the air live.

"How are you, Mayor? I'm in a little trouble," said Willie.

"Oh, what did you do Willie?"

"I said the name Barack Hussein Obama while warming up the crowd at Memorial Hall, and all hell is breaking loose."

"Oh Willie, don't worry about it. We know you. I still love you. Everything's okay."

Next, Willie and the Mayor spoke about Obama and Willie's troubles a little more. Three days later, the Mayor sent a letter to the editor of the *Cincinnati Enquirer* disavowing all knowledge of what he said to Willie earlier and publicly rebuking Willie. Weeks later, Willie and the Mayor were chosen by local WLWT Channel 5 television to talk about the Ohio election. They sat next to each other on set.

"Willie, that letter was no big deal. Don't worry about it," Mallory told Willie off the air.

"Well then, send another letter to the editor supporting me."

"No, I can't do that," Mallory said.

"Next, the Mayor tells me he's running next year for mayor and would like to have my support!," laughs Willie. "I said, Mark, let me think about it."

You have to just love politicians.

CHAPTER 44

WHOOPIE AND MORE

"Patriotism is not short, frenzied outbursts of emotions, but the tranquil and steady dedication of a lifetime."

Andrew Jackson

*E*ven the ladies jumped on the Willie recrimination bandwagon.

"That Wednesday, those left wing radical ladies on *The View*, all of whom need a man badly, took some serious shots at me. Joy Behar really enjoyed it. After the ladies ripped me for five or six minutes, Whoopie looked in the camera and told me to call her," said Willie.

Whoopie repeated the request for several days. So on Friday, Willie called her. Willie taped the interview just in case something went awry. It's something he never does. He was just not feeling very trusting anymore.

"She was warm, gracious and kind. We scheduled her to come on my show. I did mention to her that I hoped she'd gotten over the racial problems she had with Ted Danson and black face. She laughed about that," said Willie.

Ohio Congressman Rob Portman served twelve years in the House of Representatives and worked in the Bush White House as a trade representative and director of OMB. Portman has always been a friend of Willie's, and Willie always supported him. Portman introduced Willie to the President. George Bush sent Willie a handwritten note from the bus that Portman set up. Portman attended "McCain" day at Memorial Hall. There is a rumor Portman plans on running for governor in a couple of years. McCain also considered him for Vice President.

Portman has told Bush and others that, but for Willie, George Bush would not have won Ohio. In 2000 and 2004, Ohio was the swingingest swing state in the nation. It could have gone either way. In both elections, Willie actively advocated for Bush. In 2000, Willie introduced him twice, once at Devou Park and once in the City of Blue Ash. Willie went to the White House as set up by Portman. In 2004, Willie was part of group put together by the RNC to fly to Cincinnati, Dayton, Columbus and Toledo. Sean Hannity, Willie, Senator Zell Miller, Neil Bortz, and Ollie North were all together. The object was to whip up support in Ohio for Bush. We had tens of thousands coming out to the crowds. I always put on all the Bush people they wanted to put on. Portman says freely that, but for Bill Cunningham, Bush would not have been the President," Willie boasts. Despite repeated offers to do this again, the McCain campaign in 2008 did nothing.

Willie spoke to his best buddy, Sean Hannity, to put together a tour of Ohio the weekend before the election to brainstorm I-75 from Cincinnati to Toledo, stopping six to eight times along the way. With Willie as MC, Hannity would get Newt Gingrich, Ollie North, Neil Bortz and other kings of talk radio to energize the Republican base along the Ho Che Minh trial (I-75). Willie, despite profound reservations about McCain, repeatedly told the McCain campaign of the offer, explicitly. McCain turned it down. This clearly showed to Willie the stupidity of John McCain's (and his advisers) actions.

Ohio is the path to victory for any Republican President. No Republican has ever won the Presidency without Ohio. In addition, no President since John F. Kennedy won the Presidency without Ohio. The 2008 election would prove it again.

In 2004, George Bush won Ohio by only 136,483. Switching fewer than 70,000 minds would have changed the outcome. Bush received 2,796,147 votes and John Kerry received 2,659,664 votes.

McCain was risking Ohio with his treatment of Willie.

Even athletes were weighing in. Charles Barkley, on Dan Patrick's ESPN radio show, called Willie a right wing nut job. I'd like to point that Willie never had an unpaid $400,000 gambling debt.

USA Today, Newsweek, everyone reported Willie's introduction. Many readers of the local *Cincinnati Enquirer* wrote letters to the editor blasting Willie.

Many went after Willie after the McCain's introduction speech. The following are letters to the editor published by the *Cincinnati Enquirer* on March 1, 2008 and March 3, 2008.

"Warm-up" to these kinds
of family values leaves chill

The article "Cunningham's warm-up act turns McCain cold"(Feb. 27) clearly outlined for me "the party of family values" actually means to the Hamilton County Republican Party. Rob Portman and Joe Deters say that Republicans routinely invite a man to "warm *up* the crowd" whose radio show and personal appearances revolve around demeaning, racial, sexist degradation of anyone who disagrees with him. I thank the Lord that I am not a member of the party of family values!

McCain, Obama taking high road

Was it a blue moon last night? I actually agree with Peter Bronson for once ("Spanking talk radio was McCain's 'Sista Souljah' moment," Feb. 28). Sen. John McCain and Sen. Barack Obama are taking the high road. That's something Cunningham has no clue about.

Cincinnati leaders should speak out

I am not surprised at Bill Cunningham's attack on Sen. Barack Obama. I am, however, that the leadership in Cincinnati is so silent about it. It is this silence the gives our community the negative image of being intolerant. It's time that Cincinnati leadership repudiated the negativity. It is the silence that causes the distrust in the police, the justice system and a widely held feeling in minority communities that no one cares.

No place for gutter political discourse

One comment concerning the front-page article "GOP turmoil may hurt McCain (Feb. 28): If modern-day conservatives take refuge in the gutter political discourse of scoundrels like Bill Cunningham, the mantle of moral authority that they claim to carry has no merit, and the life expectancy for them as a movement is surely near its end.

Cunningham played part of clown well

I am an independent/conservative, and I am more likely to vote Republican in this election, not because I love their presumed candidate but because the Democrats scare me. I think Bill Cunningham did a credible job of assuming the role of "rodeo clown" to distract the attention from the bull that the Republican is riding.

WLW should fire Bill Cunningham

First we had Marge Schott with her racial remarks that were made known from coast to coast. Then we had racial riot in this century. Now we have Willie Cunningham, with his racist remarks about Sen. Barack Obama, on national news. We want new industry and new innovative people moving to this city. Is it any wonder why Cincinnati is not a big attraction? Don Imus was fired for similar remarks. WLW would be doing Cincinnati a favor by firing Bill Cunningham. Please, WLW, free us from Willie.

McCain, Cunningham: A Matter of Class

Sen. John McCain is a high-class guy running a high-class campaign. Willie Cunningham is a low-class guy running a low-class talk show. It doesn't get any more complicated than that.

Willie's reports from his listeners contradicted the letters to the editor.

"I don't believe I've received more than one or two calls out of 150 to 200 that are negative toward me. Everyone says McCain is a liberal. That's the viewpoint of talk radio," explains Willie.

Willie had Peter Bronson, columnist with the *Cincinnati Enquirer* on for about an hour after the McCain event. Bronson wrote an editorial that expressed Willie gave John McCain a great opportunity, a moment in the sun, so to speak, to have his Sista Soujah moment. In 1992, Sista Soujah, a female black rap star, is quoted in the *Washington Post* as saying that black people should quit killing each other for a week and start killing white people. That happened during the Clinton campaign. So Clinton went after Sista Soujah because he wanted to demonstrate to moderate Americans he was not a radical extremist. (Linguist.com states that Soujah denied the charge and her conversation was taken out of context.)

Peter Bronson wrote in his column that McCain was looking for his own Sista Soujah moment so that he could separate himself from conservative talk radio mavens like Willie in order to show liberals and independents that he will not be ruled by the Rush Limbaughs, Sean Hannitys and the Willie Cunninghams of this world. His point was that McCain, who denied meeting Willie and hadn't heard a word of what Willie said, was waiting for a moment in front of the national media where he could separate himself from conservative talk radio, because they didn't help him get to where he was.

"We're not helping him now, and we're not going to help him in the fall. So he was looking to substitute the votes from conservatives like me with moderates and liberals, which was a specific campaign philosophy," said Willie at the time.

231

CHAPTER 45

OHIO LOST

"You know why there's a Second Amendment. In case the government fails to follow the first one."

Rush Limbaugh

Willie considered John McCain's comments directed toward him to be similar to the *New York Times* story about McCain's relationship to a female lobbyist. "Unnamed sources, not knowing the facts, and making something up," explains Willie. I marveled why McCain did not adopt this position: "Hey listen. It's a local guy they used to warm up the crowd. This goes on all across the country at these rallies. He doesn't speak for me, but its no big deal." But, if Peter Bronson of the *Cincinnati Enquirer* is correct, it was simply payback time to conservative talk radio.

The John McCain "throwing Willie under the bus" incident cost McCain Ohio and the presidency. The power of 700WLW and Willie's ratings translates into influence. In another close election in Ohio, Willie's not being on board with John McCain decided the election.

Bizarre as it is, several states hold the key to winning a Presidential election: Missouri, Florida, Kentucky, Ohio, and West Virginia. They are presidential election bellwethers.

"A member of our newsroom called it the Willie effect. The effect of this will cost McCain the White House; if it does, it's on him and not me. Besides, I would prefer we have a Democrat win this year," Willie explained at the time.

Willie has publicly stated on his show the rationale for a Democrat. He sees it as a replay of 1976.

"In 1976, an Evangelical Christian farmer from Georgia with no political experience nationally or internationally ran for the presidency against a sitting president who was a moderate to liberal Republican, Gerald R. Ford. So it was Carter against Ford. Of course, Jimmy Carter won. If Ford had won in 1976, then politically, Ronald Reagan never would have existed. The air would have been taken out of the Republican Party by Gerry Ford as a moderate-to-liberal Republican. Because Carter won and helped nearly destroy the nation, it gave rise to Ronald Reagan. The country was ready for change, so they went with Ronald Reagan," explains Willie.

"The rest is history. Tax cuts. Twenty-four years of uninterrupted economic growth. The Berlin Wall comes down, defeated Communism. It's been a great quarter of a century. And Ronald Reagan never would have happened, but for Gerry Ford's defeat. And this time, if a Democrat wins the White House in November, whether it's the abomination known as Barack Hussein Obama, or the Clintonistas of Hillary Rodham Clinton, they will so fail in their presidency that the conservative movement within the Republican Party will get its sea legs and grow in 2010 and take back the Congress. Then in 2012, a Ronald Reagan will come from the heartland," Willie said before the 2008 general election.

"If, on the other hand, McCain wins, there will be no conservative within the Republican Party. He will split that party. Conservatives may form a third party and leave the Republican Party and ensure Democratic success for twenty years," Willie said at the time.

Willie threatened to support and vote for Hillary Clinton. Ann Coulter and others made similar statements. Willie actually told listeners to vote for Hillary in the primary. Hillary defeated Obama in Ohio.

He refers to Obama as an unqualified candidate, Hillary as a disqualified candidate, and McCain as a flawed candidate.

Willie also pointed to the speeches and crowds of the candidates

233

as an ominous sign. While Obama and Hillary spoke with pas-
sion before large audiences, McCain gave less than inspirational
talks to small crowds. That raised the question whether, in this
day and age of television and media, someone with McCain's lack
of speaking ability and enthusiasm can win the presidency.

"Looking back over the presidencies of the last five or six,
George Walker Bush in person is a good public speaker (I respect-
fully disagree, Willie.) At the Great American Ballpark, in Cincinnati, he had 40,000 people screaming. In Blue Ash and Devou Park,
he was extremely animated and charismatic. I think Bill Clinton
is a charismatic, touching politician whom the ladies especially
love. In today's world, with the Internet and talk radio, when Mc-
Cain speaks, he's like the luncheon speaker at the Rotary Club.
You kind of sit there, dabble with your fruit, and take a bite of
your pie, waiting for him to be done. When Obama speaks, he's
like the messiah on the mountain. I expect him to bring the fishes
and the loaves and feed the crowd. I've seen him heal the sick. The
crippled can walk and the sightless can see. That's not bad. When
Hillary spoke after her Ohio victory, it was energetic. Balloons and
confetti's going. McCain gives a speech with a teleprompter in
which he looks like death warmed over. He looked like Madeleine
Albright's husband. It's not good," explains Willie.

At sixty-nine when he took office, Ronald Reagan was supposedly old. McCain would have taken office at the age of seventy-
two.

"Because of his physical beatings and all the cancers he's had,
the guy's got Halfheimer's. I mean, he had dinner with me and
met me a couple times, been on my show. He should have said,
look, I'm not sure if I met him or not. But he said flat out, he didn't
meet me," said Willie.

"Politicians meet people all the time and do not remember all
them. I met George Bush, Sr., five or six times out at the Greater Cincinnati Airport when he came in. I was the Chairman of
the Kenton County Republican Party. The last time he came in,
he looked at me and said, "You're the guy that greets me every
time."

"I'll take him at face value. I think he's an older guy who has some failing memory, but he knows me now," laughs Willie.

Then in all ironies, Barack Obama announced on December 16, 2008, he would use his middle name, Hussein, when sworn in as President. In addition, after the general election of 2008, the corrupt Chicago-based machine, which Willie ranted about at Memorial Hall, introducing McCain, blew up. Willie was vindicated on all fronts.

Sean Hannity had Willie on his radio show on December 16, 2008 so they both could "crow" about Obama being sworn in as Barack Hussein Obama. The Democratic guest on air with Willie and Hannity, Bob Beckel, conceded the vindication.

CHAPTER 46

WILLIE'S VOTE GUIDE

"It's hard to beat a person who never gives up."

Babe Ruth

*I*mmediately prior to the elections, the *Cincinnati Enquirer*'s John Kiesewetter, who covers the media, wrote a published story with the headline "Cunningham: Hold Your Nose and Vote — Radio Host Grudgingly Backs McCain."

The following is the bulk of the article.

"Conservatives have to hold their nose and vote for McCain — not because McCain will be another Ronald Reagan, but because (Barack) Obama, will be another Jimmy Carter," says Cunningham.

Cunningham declared in February that he was done with McCain after the candidate denounced the talk host for his bombastic remarks about Sen. Barack Obama at a Memorial Hall rally. Cunningham has since warmed ever so slightly to McCain because he doesn't want more Democrats in power.

"It's sad we can't find better candidates than these two boobs. I wish we had a viable alternative. Hillary (Clinton) would be a more viable alternative," Cunningham says. "To have radical extremists like Nancy Pelosi, Barney Frank and Barack Obama seize control of the federal government would be an abomination."

Cunningham has criticized the Arizona Republican for running "the worst Republican campaign in 12 years," since Sen. Bob Dole lost to Bill Clinton in 1996.

"From my perspective, we've got to get him (McCain) to win despite himself, despite his stupidity. We've got to drag him by the ankles over the finish line. Somehow, some way," he says.

Cunningham, heard across most of Ohio on WLW, is upset that McCain's managers have rejected his suggestion to barnstorm Ohio this weekend with FOX News commentator Sean Hannity and other conservatives. Hannity, Cunningham, Oliver North, and Newt Gingrich did the same thing for Bush four years ago.

"He refuses to work with the people who put Bush over the top in 2004. We energized the Republican base the weekend before Election Day," Cunningham says.

Paul Lindsay, McCain's Ohio spokesman, declined to comment for this story.

"I understand McCain having some anger at me personally. But if he's not willing to see the value in doing this, he doesn't deserve to be president," Cunningham says.

Cunningham says his contempt for McCain is not sour grapes from McCain's swift repudiation of his performance in February. Cunningham referred to the Democrat by his full name — Barack Hussein Obama, as he does on the radio — and called him a "hack Chicago-style Daley politician."

Of course, Obama would defeat McCain in Ohio and across the country. It could have been quite different. Repeatedly on the air, Willie spoke about wanting a McCain reconciliation. It not only never happened, the McCain campaign blackballed Willie with their surrogates. Sarah Palin, Mitt Romney and others appeared on other shows on 700WLW and were not permitted to be on

Willie's by the McCain campaign. Willie had to endure mocking from Eddie and Tracy who landed many of the interviews. While Eddie and Tracy are usually having shows about who is hotter, blondes or brunettes, they were interviewing McCain surrogates while Willie was blackballed.

CHAPTER 47

NATIONAL SPOTLIGHT

"Let your hearts not be troubled."

Sean Hannity

*I*n the days that followed the 2008 Presidential election, Willie found himself mentioned by colleagues on radio and television. Rush Limbaugh pointed out on his national radio show that while McCain defended Obama and Hillary after Willie's introduction in Cincinnati, McCain failed to utter a word in defense of Sarah Palin against his staffers. McCain was throwing Sarah Palin under the bus too.

The announcement by John McCain that he had chosen Alaska Governor Sarah Palin as his running mate, was made after the noon hour on Friday, August 29, 2008. Perfect timing for Willie, who came on the air at noon. The station carried the entire introduction of Palin by McCain and then Palin's acceptance. Willie enjoyed the show. As soon as the speeches were complete, Hamilton County Prosecutor, Joe "TNT" Deters called in with a "full report."

Meanwhile, the boob Keith Olbermann made Willie the "Worst Person in the World" in October 2008. Earlier in the year, after the Barack Hussein Obama controversy, Olbermann honored Willie the first time. Olbermann, not understanding anything about Willie's show, believed Willie attacked Jews when Willie had fun on the radio with his dear friend — and Jew — Andy Furman. As a badge of honor, Keith "Obama" Olbermann has named Willie the "Worst Person in the World" at least six times.

During the October 30, 2008 broadcast of his radio show, Bill Cunningham had his buddy, Andy Furman, on the show.

The following is the transcript from the October 30 broadcast of *The Big Show* with Bill Cunningham:

CUNNINGHAM: And I guess the *L.A. Times* still has that tape in Khadidi, and doesn't release it because it's injurious to the interest of Obama. Can you imagine if the media had the tape of maybe John McCain at a Ku Klux Klan rally or at an abortion-clinic benefit and he's standing there toasting the guy who bombed the abortion clinic, and the L.A. Times wouldn't release it? What would the media do?

CUNNINGHAM: Andy Furman, how are you?

SLOAN: Why do you gotta drag me into your GOP mess? Listen, it's people like you that screwed up the Grand Old Party, OK? You racist morons, you. Because this is the year that Obama's — you do it just to twist a knife in my stomach don't you? You're just a — you like to twist the knife, and then pull it out, don't you?

CUNNINGHAM: Did you hear about this Khalidi tape where Obama is toasting a guy —

SEG DENNISON (WLW host): What?

CUNNINGHAM: — who wants to gas and fry Jews? Don't you understand? You're into self-loathing. You and your brother are *meshugana*. This Obama guy loves the PLO. Can't you figure that out?

SLOAN: You just don't (unintelligible) — you just don't like one-half-percent black people, that's your problem.

CUNNINGHAM: One-half-percent black people.

DENNISON: What the?

CUNNINGHAM: Well, Randy, we gotta go, but get back on that bus.

DENNISON: Maybe your brother will call.

CUNNINGHAM: Jews for McCain —

AUDIO CLIP: You are atrocious.

CUNNINGHAM: — because Obama wants to gas the Jews, like the PLO wants to gas the Jews, like the Nazis gassed the Jews. You got Obama introducing Arab terrorists, and the *L.A. Times* won't release the story. It is time for the Furman brothers to stand with McCain-Palin. Pay —

SLOAN: The only gas that I care about is running his mouth right now on 700WLW. That's the only gas I'm hearing.

CUNNINGHAM: I think he's talking about you, Seg.

AUDIO CLIP: Jeepers, I sure hope I don't get a gas attack.

CUNNINGHAM: He's talking about you.

DENNISON: I haven't said anything. It's you.

CUNNINGHAM: It's you

DENNISON: It's you.

CUNNINGHAM: You're the only one with gas attacks.

DENNISON: Who's talking now?

CUNNINGHAM: You.

AUDIO CLIP: Hello, sucker.

SLOAN: We need an America that represents everybody, not just the white majo– just not the white minority in this country.

CUNNINGHAM: The white minority now. We've lost already, haven't we?

DENNISON: Wow.

AUDIO CLIP: Hey.

CUNNINGHAM: Thank you very much.

SLOAN: It's over. It's over. Yes. Yes. Yes. Yes.

AUDIO CLIP: This season is over.

On December 3, 2008, Keith Olbermann named Willie a "worser" person. He did so after Willie defended the Northern Kentucky-based Creation Museum's right to believe in creationism. The Creation Museum struck a deal with the Cincinnati Zoo for a coupon deal for zoo patrons. After a few complaints, the zoo cancelled the deal. Willie was outraged at the attack on the religious group despite Willie not being a creationist. Olbermann attacked Willie and claimed he was saddled on a dinosaur. Since Willie has now earned the Olbermann label three times, he must be doing something right. Pun intended. It is also clear Olbermann must tune in to Willie's show every day.

CHAPTER 48

DRUDGE REPORT AND SEAN HANNITY

*"Bravery is the capacity to perform properly even
when scared half to death."*

General Omar Bradley

According to Premiere Radio Networks, one million people listen to Willie's national Sunday night show he does for the Drudge Report.

The Drudge Report is a U.S.-based news aggregation website run by Matt Drudge. The site consists mainly of links to stories from the U.S. and international media regarding politics, in 1994 as a weekly subscriber-based email dispatch. It is most famous for being the first news source to break the Monica Lewinsky scandal to the public after *Newsweek* decided not to publish the story.

Little was known of Matt Drudge until the Drudge Report. For many years, he took odd jobs such as night counterman at a 7-Eleven convenience store, telemarketer from Time/Life books, McDonald's manager, and sales assistant at a New York City grocery store. In 1989, he moved to Los Angeles where he took up residence in a small Hollywood apartment. He took a job in the gift shop of CBS studios, eventually working his way up to manager. It is here that he was apparently privy to some inside gossip, part of the inspiration for founding the Drudge Report. (Worried about his son's aimlessness, Drudge's father insisted on buying him a Packard-Bell computer in 1994.) The Drudge Report began as an e-mail sent out to a few friends. The original issues of the Drudge Report were part gossip and part opinion. They were distributed as an e-mail newsletter and posted to all showbiz gossip Usenet forum where they were both loved and ridiculed. In 1996, the newsletter transitioned slowly from entertainment gossip to political gossip and moved from e-mail to the web as its primary distribution mechanism.

In March 1995, the Drudge Report had 1,000 e-mail subscribers and by 1997 Drudge had 85,000 subscribers to his e-mail service. Drudge's website gained in popularity in the late 1990's after a number of reports in which he beat the mainstream media by reporting first. Drudge first received national attention in 1996 when he broke the news that Jack Kemp would be Republican Bob Dole's running mate.

The Drudge Report is 305 stations in practically every market in America. It covers geographically from Hawaii to Maine, from Alaska to Florida. Drudge put it together with Premier about three years ago, which was an extension of his web site. And he built 300 stations from ten p.m. to one a.m. Sunday night. He gave notice in July last year that he had enough. Willie believes he's making so much money from drudgereport.com that he doesn't care about paltry sums of money with the radio. Drudge notified Premier that he was quitting at the end of 2007. Willie happened to be at that time at Sean Hannity's Freedom Concert in Cincinnati.

We had to sell 10,000 tickets. It was August. It was beautiful. "It was perfect," said Willie. Willie arrived there about an hour and a half early and spent some time with Sean and his wife, Jill.

At that moment Sean Compton, who worked for Clear Channel and Premier, got an e-mail that Matt Drudge was leaving the Drudge Report at the end of the year. Willie stood with Sean Compton and Sean suggested that Willie take over the Drudge Report until the end of the year. Willie jumped. Phil Boyce is the program director of WABC in New York City, a big powerhouse AM station. Compton asked Hannity and Boyce whether they could guarantee the ABC stations. There are about ten or twelve big ABC AM powerhouses and Hannity brought the Clear Channel piece, which were about 100 stations. With everyone agreed, Sean Hannity promised Premier and Willie that he would make sure the big AMs stayed from ABC.

"But I was lucky. In October 2007, I took over and they signed me to a two-year contract," Willie said.

Willie now has a million listeners on Sunday night and about 200,000 during the week.

"I try not to be too serious and try not to be too funny. Because of John McCain, I suddenly have presence all over the country. Now I have presence and I have identity, and it's a good identity which is standing up to a liberal Republican," explains Willie.

CHAPTER 49

RADIO'S FUTURE

*"Don't waste life in doubts and fears; spend yourself
on the work before you, well assured that the right
performance of this hour's duties will be the best
preparation for the hours and ages that will follow it."*

Ralph Waldo Emerson

Willie hopes to be on the air at 700WLW for twenty more years. Radio may change, but Willie will not.

"It's going to be much more cross platforms and by platforms I mean the Internet, PDAs, cell phones. It's going to become much more on-demand. And I have to make the comment that, at some point, when you look at the logo and it says 700WLW on it, somebody is going to ask the question, what's the 700 mean? At this point, it's all about taking the product and putting it into different places. I remember when we first cut the deal with XM 173. People couldn't understand that," Darryl Parks explains.

The website is an important component of 700WLW. School closings, news, audio-video, podcasting, blogs, forums and all the rest, make an outstanding interactive experience.

"I happened to go to a convention. I remember walking into the hotel. It was right after we made the XM173 deal. Somebody came up to me and said WLW is the talk of the convention. And I wondered why," Parks said. "It was the XM association. I mean, radio is radio. I've been asked the question numerous times, why did you want to do that and why did you put WLW up on XM. I always say, do you want the short or the long answer? The short answer is putting the product everywhere I can possibly put it, and that includes XM, that includes satellite radio, that includes the Internet, that includes podcasting, that includes whatever the new technology is. That's pretty much where talk radio has to go. And that's pretty much where radio in general has to go. It has to be so much more multi — it can't be antagonistic to 700 ki-lohertz, or whatever the broadcasting frequency is. I've written articles about this — and the people look at me and they go uh, okay. The grand scheme of all this is, we have generations now (about two generations) that did not grow up on radio. So what's happening is, they're more concerned about their cell phones, the Internet, and social networking sites. To them You Tube is a tele-vision network. Many people don't realize what that is. You Tube is a television network. And what we need to do is use the new media and the new technologies which are interactive, which are to be expected to be interactive — now, talk radio is kind of an aberration," explains Darryl Parks further.

"I mean, you sit there and you listen to the music. But with talk radio, obviously there is a point of interactivity. But we have to take these new mediums, take the brand, put it into these cell phones — because we're on cell phones, and make it interactive, and try to cultivate a younger audience through these new tech-nologies. The fact of the matter is, there's going to be a day when WLW is not called WLW anymore. As wildly successful as WLW has been over the years, whether it be from the time it went on the air to 2008 — right now we have a 10 share, that means 90 percent of the people are not listening to us. Of those 90 percent, chances are more of them are going to get to listen to us because, as wildly successful as it is, WLW also has a stigma of what it is.

"So it goes back to what a caller said to Mike McConnell one time. It was an epiphany to me. A woman called up complain-ing about some double entendre topic we were doing. And her kids are in the car and, 'blah, blah, blah, my kids are forced to listen to this,' and she's complaining to Mike. And the next caller calls to say, 'Mike, I've gotta tell that woman who just called, if she's forcing her kids to listen to WLW, they hate her already.' And when you really think of it, our audience isn't kids; it's basically male," Parks said.

"Our audience is male. Outside of morning drive, it's about 70 percent male. Women are listening, but it's about 70 percent male. We over-perform within the format demographically. Our reach is much younger than the normal news talk station for a number of different reasons: The entertaining talk, the sports teams bringing in listeners to the radio station. But the reality is, if I ask a fifteen-year-old, 'Hey you want to listen to WLW?' No way! They are not going to listen. It won't interest them," said Darryl.

"But anyway, that's where radio is going; in regard to all the personalities, including Willie. Willie does video blog every day. The news department is doing a video thing every day. We did do some viral videos. The whole Brennemania thing, of two years ago, leading in to the Reds season was all about viral videos. We supported it with some billboards and obviously stadium signage, but the reality was, that was viral video and we were trying to create some talk. And what was really interesting about that was, are started hearing people repeating that back on talk show or you heard people in the stadium say Brennemania and it started picking up because we were tracking the videos. And we knew that the videos were getting a lot of views, so people were picking up on the Internet."

CHAPTER 50

SIGNING OFF

"A vote is like a rifle; its usefulness depends upon the character of the user."

Teddy Roosevelt

A s the Obama administration began its rush to cure all the "ills" of the world in one hundred days, talk radio was provided a smorgasbord of material.

The bailouts of Wall Street, the "economic" stimulus, the historical increase of the national debt and budget deficit, the move to nationalize health care, "cash for clunkers" and the general economic class energized Willie.

As expected, Willie adopted the conservative and libertarian position on all the issues. He also encouraged the populist movements such as the tea parties.

In December 2006, the county government of Kenton County, Kentucky, made a decision to build a much-needed new jail. Kenton County lies directly across the Ohio River from downtown Cincinnati. The problem with the choice of the location was that it was announced without any input from the community. It was a twenty to thirty minute drive from the Courthouse, and it was in the middle of a residential neighborhood and two tenths of a mile from a grade and middle school.

Opposition formed immediately from Independence, the town where the jail was going. Petitions were signed, protests were held, committees organized, a lawsuit was filed, a county meeting was canceled because of unruly and large crowds, boycotts and pickets were organized and alternative locations were studied.

I was part of the leadership opposing the jail because I live and work in Independence. I donated my time to the litigation and enjoyed protesting. It was great fun and drama. No one really believed our community could defeat the county's intentions.

The local media soaked up the cause, and the battle was in the news nearly every day. Before the ordeal, I didn't know Willie very well. At some point, I began calling in to Willie's show to give reports and updates on our "lost cause." Willie loved our cause and recognized it too for its entertainment value.

Here was a bunch of American citizens protesting against its government in the same manner as the Sons of Liberty protested the Stamp Act — raising hell. It was through this battle between government and the will of the people, that Willie and I became friends.

During the end of our struggle, we planned a rally on the steps of the Kenton County Courthouse in Independence, Kentucky, before and during the county meeting. Willie offered to join our mob.

On a warm and sunny fall day in 2007, Willie walked with me from my law office down the street to join the hundreds of people gathered on the Courthouse lawn with their picket signs and defiant enthusiasm.

There on a sidewalk outside the front door of the Courthouse with the crowd gathered around and without a microphone, Willie unleashed a verbal barrage in support of the people as we battled local tyranny.

He encouraged us to fight on. He yelled for us to not give up hope. He inspired us to never lose sight of our goal. In fewer than five minutes, Willie rallied the troops.

He concluded his remarks with this charge:

"Do not quit. Do not give up. Fight until the death like warrior poets in the spirit of *William Wallace!*"

The gathered throng went wild. Willie walked away to applause and jubilation. It was a moment of beauty: The Great American in a cause of liberty.

We won our battle, and the county government, to their credit, listened to the people and moved the location of the jail to a better site where it is now under construction without any protest.

Willie's goal is to be on the radio twenty more years. Considering he recently won his second Marconi award from the National Broadcasters Association as the radio personality of the year in a major market, Willie is on the top of his game. That would make him eighty-one. I don't believe Willie will work past eighty. But, that's just my opinion. Regardless, Willie loves being on the radio; it doesn't involve heavy lifting, and it's inside work. As long as there is a radio station who wants him and a microphone, Willie will be speaking truth to power as the conscience of America with the Voice of the Common Man and encouraging you, me and all Great Americans to fight to the end like warrior poets.

THERE IS A GOD

"The country is a better place because FOX News has succeeded."

Bill O'Reilly

E ach Easter, Willie's mother gave him bright, yellow marshmallow chickadees. As a boy, Mary Ellen gave each of her children something unique as a example of the distinct love she felt for each child.

In Willie's case, it continued until the day she died. Each Easter Willie received from his mother bright, yellow marshmallow chickadees. Willie's mother died on February 15, 2008, with her four children and five grandchildren at her deathbed holding her hand. It was an awful but inevitable event. Six weeks later, as Easter morning arrived, Willie walked out his driveway to pickup the Sunday paper and proceeded to his favorite leather chair in the living room. He turned to his wife and said "You know, this is the first Easter of my life with no bright yellow, marshmallow Chickadees." Penny walked over and sat on Willie's lap and they hugged each other as Willie wept. As Penny arose, Willie clicked on CBN News Sunday Morning, at the instant the TV appeared, thousands and thousands of bright yellow, marshmallow chickadees appeared on the screen and flowed toward Willie as the story of the origins of the yellow chickadees played. "Mom is still with you, and there, again, is your Easter gift," Penny remarked. That event was proof to Willie that there is a God and that his beloved mother is still with him.

ABOUT THE AUTHOR

Eric Deters is one of the top trial lawyers in America. In addition to this, he is a businessman who among other business interests is one of the principals of the national pizza chain - Snappy Tomato Pizza. He also serves as one of Willie's backups on 700WLW. He jokes that he's the "Bill Plummer to Johnny Bench."

A great lover of history, books and movies, Eric is also the author of two other books, *Pioneer Spirit* (2006) and *Saving Grace* (2006). He is currently writing a book about his brother who is afflicted with cerebral palsy entitled *Seth*, which is scheduled for release by Acclaim Press in September 2010. He's also working on a book about the challenges of practicing law.

Eric, his wife Mary, and their children, Cory, Erica, Charlie Ann, Cole, Cameron and Parker live in Independence, Kentucky near Cincinnati.

INDEX